Seasons Of Refreshing:

The Hunger For Spiritual Renewal

By

Jerry Hunt

ISBN: 1-4107-5546-0 (e-book)
ISBN: 1-4107-5545-2 (Paperback)

This book is printed on acid free paper.

All scriptures quoted, unless otherwise noted, are from the New American Standard Bible. The New Open Bible Study Edition, Thomas Nelson Publishers 1990

Front cover design by: CD Consulting; cd@labsolutions.com
Photos by: Beverly Brink

1stBooks – rev. 7/21/03

TO:

My loving wife Pat and my children: Sarah and Kris, Ryan, Rebekah, and Lindsay—thank you for your prayers and encouragement. Also, dedicated to the Upper Room Small Church Class, at Nappanee Missionary Church, for their love and devotion to the Word of God.

SPECIAL THANKS TO:

Pastor Dave Engbrecht for his input and writing the Forward and a special thanks to my daughter, Rebekah, for her editorial skills and assistance.

Table of Contents

PART 3:

EPILOGUE

How Then Should We Live?

Forward:

Every one of us faces times of spiritual barrenness and even though it is inevitable that they will come, it is critical that we know the clear path to "times of refreshing."

We cannot always control what happens to us, however, we can control our response. In order to sustain us in the midst of dry times, it is important for us to develop "habits of the heart." As you embark on this study, you need to understand two things about the author. First, you will see his love of the Bible and his desire to have God's truth penetrate lives. Over the past ten years, I have watched Jerry faithfully teach God's Word. Weekly, he opens the Word of God and mines its deep truths. His depth of study provides solid food for his students. It could truly be said of Jerry, "he's a man of one book;" a superb Bible teacher. There is an added benefit to having this teaching in book form. Sometimes sitting under Jerry in the classroom is like drinking from a fire hydrant. Now you have the opportunity to drink at your own pace.

More than just mining the truths, Jerry is taking you on a journey to apply them. This is not about theory or mere accumulation of facts—it is about taking and applying God's Word to our lives and making it work. Our moral compass, in the midst of desert seasons, is God's Word. Mere knowledge is not sufficient in dry times; it is the application of that knowledge that becomes key. That is what you will discover in this study.

Secondly, you need to understand Jerry's love for what I call "authentic spiritual community." Frankly, this is simply "doing church God's way!" A part of our strength for dry times is a connectedness that comes from being a part of a spiritual family. For Jerry, that family is called "THE UPPER ROOM," a body of nearly a hundred people that gather weekly to practice "community" and study the Word. This body of believers genuinely cares for each other and I have witnessed their compassion. They practice a ministry of presence when a family member has died, they model encouragement when someone has lost a job, they pray for each other in times of sickness and discouragement, and they laugh together and know how to enjoy life. Truly, they practice what they teach! As Jerry's pastor, I have learned much about "pastoring" from him.

It is time for each of us to take the first step on a journey to personal revival and seasons of refreshing. If this were a race, it would be said, "Gentlemen, start your engines." If it were a missile launch, it would be said, "We have lift-off." The bottom line is simple, personal revival—seasons of refreshing—begins now!

Dave Engbrecht
Senior Pastor
Nappanee Missionary Church
Nappanee, Indiana

Introduction:

Seasons of refreshing, the hunger for spiritual renewal is our focus as we learn how to develop a closer, more intimate relationship with the LORD Jesus Christ. Seasons of refreshing are described in Acts 3:19, where the apostle Peter states, *"Repent therefore and return, that your sins may be wiped away, in order that times of refreshing may come from the presence of the Lord."* Seasons of refreshing consist of those times of spiritual renewal or personal revival—a returning to our first love, Jesus Christ.

To use the word "return" implies that we have left someone or something. Perhaps it is not a question of leaving so much as it is a question of "neglection." We often become preoccupied with the tyranny of the urgent and neglect the important. Sometimes we neglect our spouse, our children, our friends, but most of the time we neglect our relationship with the LORD. We may "do" devotions, or go to a Bible study in order to "maintain" our relationship with God—but maintenance is not growth! Lou Holtz, the former head coach of the Notre Dame Football team, in a speech in South Bend, Indiana commented on why he left the University. *"I wasn't tired of coaching,"* he said, *"I was tired of maintaining."* (1) This same difficulty happens in our relationship with God. We try "maintaining" instead of growing, and the result is sliding backwards. The purpose of this book is to renew or return to times of intimacy with our LORD and to experience continual seasons of refreshing from His presence.

The Apostle Paul commands us in Ephesians 5:18 to be filled with the Holy Spirit. This is a moment-by-moment walk— a surrender to His power and control over our lives. It is a yielding to His Lordship, literally a "dying of self." When we take control over our own lives and walk according to the flesh, we walk contrary to God's will. We desire God's presence and power within and want to live a life pleasing to Him; yet, the practice is not always there. There is the constant struggle with the flesh and many times, the flesh wins! The reason why the flesh wins out over the Spirit is that we desire it to. We choose to sin and walk contrary to God's Word, and then wonder why God's presence and power is lacking within our lives, our church body, and literally our nation.

We have attended seminars, conferences, special meetings, and revival crusades in order to have a closer walk with God. Then, after a few days, we return to the same lifestyle that we had before the meetings. This, Peter likens to a dog returning to his vomit or to a sow, once washed, returning to the mire. (2) Sounds disgusting, however, this illustration God wants to plant within our thoughts, so we will not return to the same lifestyle we were delivered.

Apathy is a killer of all growing businesses. It is also the silent killer of many relationships; whether this being marriages, a growing church body, or an individual believer.

Apathy can creep into one's life quietly and be unnoticed for years. It is a loss of desire for the things of God, a developing of a cold and distant heart. It presents itself in prayerlessness, in ignoring God's Word, in rejection of fellowship with other believers, and in a lifestyle that leads to emptiness and frustration with life. God has put within each of us a God-shaped vacuum only He can fill. We can try to fill that vacuum with things, a career, money, job status, etc., but they will never satisfy. God desires an intimate relationship with us because He loves us and longs for our fellowship. He desires to fill us with His presence and to grant seasons of refreshing if we will return to Him.

Regaining that intimacy begins with the acknowledgement we are desperately in need of God's forgiveness and His revival in our hearts. It will mean to seek Him again in His Word. God told the nation of Israel, through Jeremiah the prophet, *"You will seek Me and find Me, when you search for Me with all your heart. And I will be found by you."* (Jeremiah 29:13-14). This is the promise we have, if we seek Him we will indeed find Him, and be found by Him. It also involves returning to the promises that are available to us. God told the nation of Israel, *"Stand by the ways and see and ask for the ancient paths, Where the good way is, and walk in it; And you shall find rest for your souls"* (Jeremiah 6:16). God is asking us to return to the paths of righteousness; to again be filled with the Holy Spirit and enjoy times of refreshing from the presence of the

LORD. This is what a season of refreshing is about—the hunger for spiritual renewal.

Throughout the text, you will notice the use of the word "LORD" in this spelling, versus the traditional "Lord." I have done this as a reference to the Hebrew name *"Yahweh"* (YHWH) out of reverence for the Holy name of God.

Part One: The Desperation for Seasons of Refreshing.

Desperation:

1. The condition of being desperate.
2. Recklessness arising from despair.

(The American Heritage Dictionary)

Desperate is:

- When you are tired of the emptiness and frustration of life.
- When you have had enough of exchanging the tyranny of the urgent at the sacrifice of the important.
- The heart's cry for God's presence in your life.
- Coming to the end of yourself and the beginning of God.
- Longing to see the fire of God fall and consume you as the living sacrifice.
- Wanting to see a move of God resulting in the lost being saved.
- The acknowledgement that apart from Him I can do nothing.
- Being broken for the things that break God's heart.
- Seeing yourself in the light of God's Holiness.
- Wanting God to restore your marriage and bring healing to your relationship.
- When you have lost everything but God.
- Longing to see your children walk with God.

- A broken spirit praying for broken lives to be healed and forgiven.
- The heart's cry for personal revival.

"My God, my God, why hast Thou forsaken me? Far from my deliverance are the words of my groaning. O my God, I cry by day, but Thou dost not answer; And by night, but I have no rest."

"Be not far from me, for trouble is near; For there is none to help. Yet Thou art holy, O Thou who art enthroned upon the praises of Israel. In Thee our fathers trusted; They trusted, and Thou didst deliver them. To Thee they cried out, and were delivered; In Thee they trusted, and were not disappointed." (Psalm 22:1-5)

Chapter 1

The Need for Seasons of Refreshing.
Where Are We?

Lost in America:

A couple asked the young boy along the side of the road, the direction to the nearest town. The boy quickly responded, "Just follow that road." He pointed to the crossroads and said, "It will take you there." Grateful for the boy's directions, the couple headed off in that direction. The road on which they were traveling first turned into a gravel road, then a dirt path, and finally dead-ended in a cow pasture. The couple was officially lost in America. What the boy didn't tell them was that they were heading in the wrong direction! Sound familiar? We often travel down roads in the wrong direction thinking the destination we are looking for is just over the next hill. We have traveled along, looking and hoping, often too stubborn to stop and ask for directions, until we too, are lost in America. I'm afraid to admit I have done this numerous times. I have thought that I'd found a shortcut, but it only led me farther and farther away from my destination.

Recently, I was invited to a dinner meeting to discuss future business plans. The host gave me directions to the restaurant where we were to meet along with the time of the meeting.

However, on the way, I must have taken a wrong turn, because I was lost! I called up my friend, who was hosting the dinner, and told him of my predicament. The first question he asked was, "Where are you now?" I told him the name of the intersection and from there he gave detailed instructions on how to find my way to the restaurant. We have all been lost on occasion, and have been asked, "Where are you, now?" We try to describe, to the best of our abilities, where we are in order to get back to familiar ground. Once finding our way, there is a sense of relief, and we can continue with the journey.

Our spiritual life is often like that. We have traveled down wrong roads in the wrong direction, which only led us further away from our destination. We have become frustrated and angry at our situation, wondering what happened along the way. And we blame others for not providing accurate or updated directions to keep us from getting lost. Instead of blaming others, however, we need to admit to ourselves we have turned onto the wrong road. Whether intentionally or accidentally, not knowing when it necessarily happened, but we are lost and in desperate need of finding our way back.

In our spiritual journey to seasons of refreshing, we begin with an understanding of where we are now. Realizing that the road we are traveling on, either is leading us to a more intimate walk with Jesus Christ, or is taking us away from His presence. Either we are enjoying seasons of refreshing from the presence of the LORD, or we are struggling with emptiness and frustration. Like any travelers asking for directions, the first question is "Well, where are we now?"

A Spiritual Evaluation:

"Where are we," is a good question to ask God! If we are to see the need for seasons of refreshing in our lives, we must each begin with an honest examination of our personal walk with God. Are we on the right road and heading in the direction leading us to our desired destination? The Psalmist, David, asked that question when he cried out, *"Search me, O God, and know my heart; Try me and know my anxious thoughts; And see if there be any hurtful way in me, And lead me in the everlasting way.* (1) David asked God to search him and examine his thoughts, motives, and actions, checking to see if they were pure, holy, and on the right road. When David asked God to "know my heart," he had invited God into his inner conscience, where nothing was hidden and where all had been laid bare. When God begins to shine His spotlight of truth on our inward man it can become very revealing and humbling. Yet, David's cry was that nothing hurtful nor wicked would be in his life to grieve the heart of God. His desire was for God to lead him in the *"everlasting way"* on the right roads of life. David longed for seasons of refreshing in the presence of the LORD. In asking God to examine his heart, David wanted to make sure he was on the right road of his spiritual journey.

Our spiritual journey, like David's, begins with soul searching. We ask God to search our hearts and know our thoughts, to point out the secret sins we so often hide. He examines us and we listen.

In asking, "Where are we," can best be answered by the spiritual examination below. Take time alone with God too carefully ponder these questions and your own answers.

Questions to meditate on:

1. **How much time do I spend daily in God's Word?**
    A. Much. B. Fair.   C. Little. D. None.

2. **I can honestly say that prayer is a delight for me, and I enjoy spending time alone with God.**
    A. Yes.   B. No.

3. **I enjoy daily times of worship of God.**
    A. Yes.   B. No.

4. **I look forward to attending my church and fellowshipping with other believers.**
    A. Yes.   B. No.

5. **My Sunday School hour is important to me, therefore, it is a priority in my life.**
    A. Yes.   B. No.

6. **I long for the presence and the power of God in my life, and have made myself available for His use.**
    A. Yes.   B. No.

7. **I take time to be silent before God in order for Him to examine my life, and point out areas that need His forgiveness and cleansing.**

   A. Yes.   B. No.

8. **I have a burden for the lost, and spend time praying for them.**

   A. Yes.   B. No.

9. **I am willing to be used of God no matter where or how.**

   A. Yes.   B. No.

10. **I strive to be a growing Christian.**

    A. Yes.   B. No.

These are tough questions to answer because they all have to do with time. In today's world, time is the most precious of commodities. It takes time to develop intimacy with someone you love and you should willingly sacrifice time for your wife or husband. Developing an intimacy with God isn't any different. In drawing close to Him, we must be willing to sacrifice the time to do so. For many people, time is least available, and the hardest resource to give. Our schedules are full! Because of the demands on our time, we are constantly feeling empty and frustrated with life.

The Emptiness and Frustrations of Life:

I did a seminar on Time Management and asked the question, "Over the next five years do you see yourself

> *Like the commercial said, "You only go around once in this life, so go for all the gusto you can." Only this "gusto" has left children without fathers, husbands without wives, and infants without mothers to care for and nurture them.*

becoming more busy and putting in longer hours than you do now, or do you see yourself as doing less?" Their response was, "more busy and longer hours." Whatever happened to the forty-hour workweek? I thought we were supposed to end up with more free time and less stress? The demands on our time have increased, and with those demands, came added pressures, more responsibilities, and increasing stress levels. And when we could not meet all of those demands, emptiness and frustration set in.

More and more people are feeling empty and frustrated with life. In spite of vast amounts of income at their disposal, they still cannot buy that which will give meaning and purpose to their lives. They have found the more they spend, the less happy they become. They are empty and frustrated because they have sacrificed everything for their career, and the rewards have failed to provide happiness.

Emptiness and frustration with life is the result of a selfish, self-seeking attitude, a lifestyle that has sacrificed family, friends, and relationships in order to get ahead. Like the commercial says, "You only go around once in this life, so go for all the gusto you can." Only this "gusto" has left children without fathers, husbands without wives, and infants without mothers to care for and nurture them.

The emptiness and frustration with life can only be satisfied when we willingly submit to the Lordship of Jesus Christ. Then, we begin to see how empty our existence is without Him. Greed and selfishness often determine our frustration level. We need to remember the axiom, which states; "Only one life, so soon is past; only what's done for Christ will last." What matters most in life can only be found in a relationship with Jesus Christ. Where are we? We're in need of seasons of refreshing, a returning to a personal revival with God.

The Tyranny of the Urgent:

We live in the tyranny of the urgent! We have schedules to keep, places to go and people to see, and plenty of projects to do. Which all have to be done, **now!** We put in long hours adding more stress to our lives, all in the name of "making a living." I have watched the corporate cycle of people who sacrificed anyone and anything in order to climb to the top, only to lose the position for which they were striving to someone else more eager and willing to pay an even greater price. For example, Bob moved 19 times in 21 years to accept various positions within his company. Recently, when profits turned down, Bob was downsized out of the company. What does he have to show for his 19 moves and 21 years of sacrifice for the tyranny of the urgent? A family that doesn't know him, nor has the experience of a stable home, school, church, or even lasting friendships with neighbors. This story can be told repeatedly as so many have sacrificed their marriages, families, and friendships for the "big promotion" and the ever-elusive status symbol of success.

There is nothing wrong with the drive to succeed. However, when one becomes driven for the purposes of wealth, power, and privilege, the price of success can become enormous. Jesus once said, *"Where your treasure is, there will your heart be also."* (4) Have our "treasures" become the very things the world seeks after and deem as important? We have all seen the bumper sticker stating, "He who has the most toys when he dies, wins." Yet, what has been won? Bigger houses, faster cars, newer games, and greater toys usually lead to bigger debts. Jesus said, *"For what does it profit a man to gain the whole world, and forfeit his soul?" "For what shall a man give in exchange for his soul?"* (5) What is the price tag for achieving success in the world's eyes? It is the loss of one's own soul and a very high price indeed!

> *We have over-scheduled our lives in the same way an airline company would over-book a flight.*

Recently, my friend Dan left a very lucrative job with a promising career in order move his family to Tanzania, Africa to be a missionary. His family's mission is to work with the local Lutheran Church giving direction in finances and teaching the word of God. Many thought it was a big mistake for Dan to give up his future and security to move to Africa. Yet, Dan's treasure is to do the will of God; *"For where your treasure is, there your heart will be also."* Jim Elliot, missionary to the Auca Indians in Ecuador, made this statement, which continues to speak to hearts everywhere, *"He is no fool to give up what he cannot keep, to gain what he cannot lose."* (6) Jim Elliot, along with four of his friends, would later die at the hands of those to whom he came to minister. He did give up what he could not keep and gained what he could not lose.

When we come home from work, the challenges on our time only increases. Once again, we have schedules to keep, places to go, and projects to do. The strains on family time are enormous. We are deluged with school functions, sports programs, recitals, practices, and youth activities at church. The concept of a family meal together has become a thing of the past. Family bonding around the dinner table is now a grab-and-go few minutes of conversation as we hurry to the next event. Our calendars are full! We have over-scheduled our lives in the same way an airline company over-books a flight. When forced to cancel an obligation, we have the overwhelming feelings of guilt.

The tyranny of the urgent has put massive amounts of stress on individuals today. Canadian scientist Hans Selye, after forty years of research on stress, discovered the body's adaptive response to stress could be surmised in three phases. Phase 1: you experience an *alarm reaction* due to the sudden activation of your sympathetic nervous system. You mobilize resources, your heart rate starts to zoom and blood is diverted to your skeletal muscles, and you feel the faintness of shock. Phase 2: you try to fight the challenge with *resistance* by coping with the stressor. Your temperature, blood pressure, and respiration remain high, and there is a sudden outpouring of hormones. If persistent, the stress may eventually deplete your body's reserves. Phase 3: *exhaustion* sets in as energy reserves are depleted. You are more vulnerable to illness or even, in extreme cases, collapse and death. Selye's basic point is this; prolonged stress can produce physical deterioration. [7] In another related study, it was found six out of ten people said they felt they were under "great stress" at least once a week. [8] Scientific evidence point's stress is a contributing factor to coronary heart disease, psychosomatic illnesses, and even certain cancers. [9]

Where are we? The tyranny of the urgent has produced a compromising lifestyle by exchanging the important for the unimportant of life. Too often, we work long hours to buy the things we don't need to impress people we don't like and to live a life where we are not happy.

Time is more Precious than Money:

> *We often use the excuse, for our limited time we spend with our children, that quality is more important than quantity. Don't kid yourself, quantity dictates the quality of time spent!*

It is said that people today would rather give money than time. Time is very precious, it is limited to just twenty-four hours a day, and to seven days a week. It is hard to obtain and more difficult to give. We often use the excuse, for our limited time we spend with our children, that quality is more important than quantity. Don't kid yourself; quantity dictates the quality of time spent!

Where are our priorities when it comes to time? Jim leaves his house early Monday morning to travel extensively in his role as a salesperson. He returns home late Friday afternoon exhausted from the long week. Saturday, he spends much of the day playing golf with his friends in order to "relax." When asked about his priorities in life, he is quick to respond that his family is first. Yet, you couldn't tell that by the amount of time he actually spends with them. Our actions often betray our words.

We say the important things in life are our family, our fellowship with believers, and our relationship with God. However, that is not where the focus of our time is spent. Again, Jesus said, *"For where your treasure is, there will be your heart also."* (10) The priority of our treasure, meaning something of great worth is where the focus of our time is spent. The problem is, our treasure is often that which does not satisfy, and leaves us empty and frustrated with life.

Where are you? Has the tyranny of the urgent created massive amounts of stress in your life? Are you empty and frustrated, struggling to make sense of your existence? Maybe you have focused on the wrong priorities, which in turn have led to wrong attitudes and wrong relationships. Are you on the wrong road?

During times of turmoil, we often ask God why He has allowed this crisis to happen. Why has He made life so hard? Why does He remain silent when we call out for help? Like the Psalmist David cried out, *"My God, My God why hast Thou forsaken me?"* Has God really forsaken us or have we forsaken God? Is there a need for times of refreshing in your life?

In the scriptures, the Psalmist David experienced the same emptiness and frustration with life as we all have experienced. He spent years wandering and hiding from King Saul, who sought to take his life. Friends forsook him; his enemies planned to destroy him. David felt overwhelmed in his circumstances, as if God had forsaken him. He suffered the physical affects of stress and anguish, and wondered why God was silent during his times of trouble. Yet, God allowed those trials in David's life in order to draw him back to seasons of refreshing from the presence of the LORD. Let's look at David's cries of anguish as we, too, struggle with those feelings.

The Cries of Anguish:

"My God, my God, why hast Thou forsaken me? Far from my deliverance are the words of my groaning. O my God, I cry by day, but Thou dost not answer; And by night, but I have no rest" (Psalm 22:1-2).

I. The First Lament: Why has God Forsaken Me?

This expression of despair and hopelessness are David's cry for direction back to the right road he was once on. He had the feeling of being abandoned by God—being left all alone to face the overwhelming circumstances of life. Like a rat in a maze, everywhere he turned, there was no escape. The tyranny of the urgent had exhausted him, and he felt hopeless in a helpless situation.

Hopelessness is a devastating emotion. Especially when a person feels trapped in a situation where there appears to be no way out. He is without hope due to circumstances surrounding him and is in total despair. God seems distant, far off, and uncaring. In his heart, he is asking, "Why has God forsaken me when I need Him the most?"

The tyranny of the urgent can make one feel like he is on a merry-go-round with no way of getting off. The emptiness and frustration of life can leave one with feelings of hopelessness, and like David, asking God why He has forsaken him. We have created similar situations by buying the lifestyle the world has sold. We choose to go down the wrong roads that lead to emptiness and frustration. We focus our lives on money, prestige, and power, thinking these things will satisfy the emptiness. We live to please self no matter what the cost may be to others or to ourselves. In the process, we grieve God's Spirit and He withdraws from us. We continue on, living our own selfish lifestyle, until it all comes crashing down on top of us. Then, we ask God why He has forsaken us?

However, God didn't forsake David, nor has He forsaken us. He is right where we have left Him, on His throne and in complete control. When we become desperate for seasons of refreshing in our live, then we will return to Him.

II. The Second Lament: Why is God Silent?

"O my God, I cry by day, but Thou dost not answer; And by night, but I have no rest" (Psalm 22:2).

The cry of anguish is, "Where is God when I hurt?" David, in his anguish, cried out to God, but He was silent. Sometimes, God is very vocal in His silence! God was teaching David to trust Him patiently. In our situation, God's silence may be a shout for us to return to the road leading back to Him. God's silence doesn't mean He is uncaring, or unwilling to hear the cries of His children. He, often times, is working behind the scenes bringing about His purpose and plan for our life. The believers in Christ have the promise that God will never leave nor forsake them (Hebrews 13:5). No matter how difficult the road, or how tough the trial, we have the assurance that God's Word is true, and He is faithful.

The Apostle Paul wrote, *"He who did not spare His own Son, but delivered Him up for us all, how will He not also with Him freely give us all things?"* (12) God went to great lengths to show us His love, by offering up His dear Son. Shouldn't that provide the hope that He will see us through the dark times we face? Paul asks, in Romans 8:35, what or who shall separate us from the love of Christ? Paul then points out seven events he has been through and knows first hand of the deliverance in Christ. He asks, *"Shall tribulation"* separate us? In other words, will times of great tension or stress keep us from the love of Christ? Shall *"distress"* separate us? Meaning, times of uncertainty and anxiety due to circumstances beyond our control. Shall *"persecution"* separate us? Meaning, will times of being ridiculed and suffering hardship for the cause of Christ keep us from Christ's love? Will *famine,* separate us? Meaning, facing times of shortages or without the basic needs of life, will that separate us? Will *"nakedness"* separate us from the love of Christ? Meaning, being exposed to the raw elements of nature, does it mean Christ's love no longer touches us? Will *"peril"* separate us? In other words, when we face life-threatening situations, has He forsaken us? Will the *"Sword,"* separate us? Meaning, when we face death, is He there for us? Yet, in all these things, Paul triumphantly states we are more than conquerors through Him who loved us (Romans 8:37). The battle has already been fought, the outcome has been determined, and we are the victors! The child of God has the promise that God has not, cannot, and will not forsake His own!

Why is God sometimes silent? He often uses the emptiness and frustrations we are going through as a way of calling us back to Him. When we come to the end of ourselves, we begin to realize how desperate we are for God again in our lives. God often lets us go through the dark valley in order for us to see our great need for Him. Sometimes, it takes a tragedy, a trial, or times of great stress in our lives to drive us to our knees and cry out for His help. Like He taught David, He is also teaching us to trust in Him. God may appear to be silent, but He is working on our behalf. During the times of silence, He is asking us to trust Him and to walk by faith. God will supply the grace for us to do just that, if we will let Him.

God has not and cannot forsake His own! He is not silent or passive on our behalf. However, when we become so preoccupied with the tyranny of the urgent, when we are too busy to meet with God, He will remain silent until we acknowledge our need and return to Him.

David asked why God had forsaken him and why He had remained silent. Both of these questions were cries of anguish from a troubled heart. Due to the stress he was under, David began to experience physical side effects. In Psalm 22, David described what he was going through as a result of the strain he was under. We often go through these same physical effects of stress and at times, they can be devastating.

The Fruits of Anguish:

"I am poured out like water, And all my bones are out of joint; My heart is like wax; It is melted within me. My strength is dried up like a potsherd, And my tongue cleaves to my jaws; And Thou dost lay me in the dust of death" (Psalm 22:13-15).

"I am poured out like water."

This verse typifies the suffering of Jesus Christ on the cross and the devastating physical and psychological affects of anguish and stress. Being poured out like water is to be drained of all our strength. We are exerting and expending all our energies, leading us to the point of sheer exhaustion. The fountain of tears has been opened and poured out until there is nothing left to bring forth. One has become tired and worn out mentally, emotionally, and spiritually. Are you poured out like water? Have you given of your time and energy until there is nothing left to offer? The demands of job, home, and family have exacted all they can and there is nothing more to give. The hope we have is to be filled again with the "living water," which only comes from Jesus Christ.

"And all my bones are out of joint."

This is the feeling of being forcibly stretched to the point of breaking. David was being pulled in every direction by conflicts and problems that did not have simple answers. The demands on his time and attention to details were needed, and were the very things He did not have to give. You too, may be pulled in many directions, not knowing where to begin first. The stress and tension of this "pulling" rips into the very fiber of your being and you become "out of joint" or literally out of sorts with everybody around you. You end up striking out at everyone, rather than taking the conflicts to the One who can solve them and bring a healing within. Being pulled in every direction will eventually rip you apart like a teddy bear in a tug-of-war. The only mending that can put you back together is to return to Jesus Christ and seek His healing.

"My heart is like wax."

The melting of the heart is experiencing the fire of anguish and the heat of suffering. The courage to resist and stay strong in the face of adversity is gone. The heart, or inner being, is on the verge of giving up and is in despair. Fear has taken over and you become weak and timid. Paul, in his letter to young Timothy stated; *"For God hath not given us the spirit of fear; but of power, and of love, and of a sound mind."* (13) Fear looks at circumstances and asks, "Where is God?" Faith responds to circumstances and says, "God is able!" God has given us power, which is the ability to stand in His strength. He has given us His love in order to strengthen and encourage us and He has given us a sound mind, which is the ability to apply wisdom in every situation. If your heart has become like wax, take courage, God is in the strengthening business.

"My strength is dried up."

The ability to stand in faith is gone! There is nothing left to give as exhaustion and hopelessness take their toll. Does this describe where you are—tired, exhausted, and worn out with the daily pressure of life, unable to find the strength to go on? The writer of the book of Hebrews explains what to do in such circumstances, *"Let us therefore draw near with confidence to the throne of grace, that we may receive mercy and may find grace to help in time of need."* (14) God is in the grace-giving business, and when our strength is gone, His is beginning.

"Thou dost lay me in the dust of death."

David was poured out, stretched to the limit, fearful, and physically exhausted. He was helpless, hopeless, and desperate, feeling as though there was nothing left to live for. Many of us have faced these same kinds of emotions.

What are the solutions to these problems? How can we find hope in a seemingly hopeless situation? How do we get off of the merry-go-round we are on and concentrate more on the important issues of life? Let's look at the cries of hope to see how God brings about seasons of refreshing within David.

The Cries of Hope:

"Yet Thou art holy, O Thou who art enthroned upon the praises of Israel. In Thee our fathers trusted; They trusted, and Thou didst deliver them. To Thee they cried out, and were delivered; In Thee they trusted, and were not disappointed" *(Psalm 22:3-4).*

I. Remember Who God Is.

"Yet, Thou art holy, O Thou who art enthroned upon the praises of Israel."

God is holy and righteous in all that He is or does. There is "no shadow of turning with Him." His Word, can be counted on and trusted when everything around fails. David realized God never left him. He remembered that God has always been enthroned in the praises of Israel. God inhabits praise! When we begin to praise Him, we experience His presence anew in our lives. The stress and tension from the trials we are in begins to fade. When we praise Him, He fills our life with His peace and gives us His hope and courage. The emptiness and frustrations of life are removed and in their place is the filling of the Holy Spirit.

David continued in his praise by stating, *"In Thee our fathers trusted; They trusted and Thou didst deliver them."* (v. 4) In times past, God heard the cries of His children and delivered them. God was faithful in the past, He is faithful now, and He will be faithful in the future. David recalled God's faithfulness throughout Israel's history. They trusted—God delivered them—in spite of the overwhelming circumstances. When faced with difficulties, we need to reflect on the deliverance of God in our lives and we too, will likewise break into praise.

The cry of David's heart was a plea for God (verse 19) to *"be not far off, O Thou my help."* The meaning was for God to be close by—ready to rescue, just as He had done in the past. God is closer to us than the air we breathe, He is not far off. However, He will wait to hear from us! David, in his praise and worship of God, began to plead for deliverance and God moved. When we are willing to praise and exalt our God, hope fills us and He provides seasons of refreshing. However, are we willing to cry out to Him for help?

II. Stand in Awe of Him:

"I will tell of Thy name to my brethren; In the midst of the assembly I will praise Thee. You who fear the LORD, praise Him; All you descendants of Jacob, glorify Him, And stand in awe of Him, all you descendants of Israel. For He has not despised nor abhorred the affliction of the afflicted; Neither has He hidden His face from him; But when he cried to Him for help, He heard" (Psalm 22:22-24).

"I will tell of Thy name."

Because of God's deliverance, David would continually tell the story of God's faithfulness. David had many ordeals where God delivered him from Saul. Yet, in his anguish he turned to the only hope he had, the Holy One of Israel. As you reflect in where you are in your spiritual evaluation, do you remember the joy you had after you were saved? The excitement you experienced after coming to know the LORD Jesus Christ and began growing in Him? That excitement boiled over and you told everybody in sight, remember? You boldly proclaimed what great things God did in your life. What happened to that excitement? Do you still tell the story of God's faithfulness? Do you see the need to experience personal revival?

"I will praise thee."

David proclaimed this as a time of worship and returning to the God who delivered and sustained him. *"I will praise thee in the midst of the assembly,"* that is, to speak to one another in psalms and hymns and spiritual songs, singing and making melody with your heart to the LORD (Eph. 5:19). To praise the LORD is an act of worship from a repentant heart. A heart filled with the love of Christ and wanting to praise and worship Him. Praise is an act of faith and will lift your Spirit even in times of great distress. Second Chronicles 20 is a beautiful story of deliverance, King Jehoshaphat, faced with overwhelming odds against a multitude of armies, began to pray and seek God's help. God responded by telling all of Judah and King Jehoshaphat, *"Do not be afraid of this great multitude, for the battle is not yours, but God's"* (v.15). Then King Jehoshaphat did strange thing. He appointed the local choir to lead the army of

Israel into war. It's hard to imagine that a King would appoint his choir members to lead the charge rather than the best-trained, highly elite fighters. However, note the song they were singing, *"Give thanks to the LORD, for His lovingkindness is everlasting"* (v.21). Scriptures record, *"When they began singing and praising, the LORD set ambushes against the sons of Ammon, Moab, and Mount Seir, who had come against Judah; so they were routed."* When the Israelites began to sing and praise the LORD, God brought about a great victory. If we will learn to praise Him, to glorify God for all He has done and will do, God can and will bring about a great deliverance in and through us.

"And stand in awe of Him."
David after asking why God had forsaken him now responds in praise and worship of Him, literally standing in awe of His presence. When we begin to praise, God works in and through us. We stand in awe of what He has done, from the deliverance we just read about with King Jehoshaphat, to the change of heart He brings to us. When the Psalmist David began to worship and praise God, he renewed his faith and confidence in the LORD and began to experience seasons of refreshing.

The Application:

Acts 3:19 states, *"Repent therefore and return, that your sins may be wiped away, in order that times of refreshing may come from the presence of the LORD."* To *"repent"* is to examine where you are and turn from that lifestyle. It is a change of heart, an acknowledgment of your need for God to fill again your life with the presence of His Holy Spirit. Remember the spiritual evaluation you did? The thought emphasized was about time and seeing the need for personal revival. Repentance is making time for the "important," it is a change of priorities. When David was willing to take the time to worship and praise God, and to get his eyes off of "the tyranny of the urgent," God began to bring times of refreshing into his life. *"For He has not despised nor abhorred the affliction of the afflicted; Neither has He hidden His face from him; But when he cried to Him for help, He heard"* (v. 24). In your struggle to manage priorities, in times of anguish, God has not hidden His face from you. This is the source of comfort, knowing God sees your need and hears your cry and will again fill you with His presence, just as He did with David.

"Repent therefore and return." To *"return"*, is to come back to where you once were. A time when you were sensitive to the LORD's moving in your heart and a time when you met with Him in prayer and study of His Word. Do you remember that time? It is not a question of "My God, My God, why has Thou forsaken me?" It is a question of when and how did "I" forsake God in my life. It is realizing that it is "I" who moved and not God. Repentance and returning are the key ingredients to seeing the need for a season of refreshing.

"That your sins may be wiped away." If you will ask, God will forgive and cleanse as He always has. The result will be times of refreshing that will come from being within the presence of the LORD. When you desire those times, you will again experience the joy of His salvation and the fresh filling of the Holy Spirit.

You have taken a good look at where you are and the need for a season of refreshing to fill your life. Perhaps it is time to acknowledge your need to God, to have Him search your heart and point out areas that need to be confessed and repented of, so He may again restore joy into your life.

In closing of this chapter, I am reminded of an old hymn of dedication written by Adelaide Pollard entitled, *Have Thine Own Way, Lord!* Let this be your prayer as you read these words.

Have Thine own way, Lord! Have Thine own way!
Thou art the Potter; I am the clay
Mould me and make me after Thy will.
While I am waiting, Yielded and still.

Have Thine own way, Lord! Have Thine own way!
Search me and try me, Master today!
Whiter than snow, Lord, Wash me just now,
As in Thy presence, Humbly I bow.

Have Thine own way, Lord! Have Thine own way!
Wounded and weary, Help me, I pray!
Power all power Surely is Thine!
Touch me and heal me, Savior divine! (14)

Recall & Application

1. In what ways are you experiencing the "emptiness and frustration of Life?"

_____

_____

2. Describe how the "tyranny of the urgent" affects you?

_____

_____

3. Why did David feel that God had forsaken him?

_____

_____

4. Why is God sometime silent when you pray?

_____

_____

5. When you begin to praise God, what happens in your spirit?

_____

_____

6. When God speaks, do I listen? God spoke to me in the following ways:

_____

_____

As the deer pants for the water brooks, So my soul pants for Thee, O God. My soul thirsts for God, for the living God; When shall I come and appear before God? My tears have been my food day and night, While they say to me all day long, "Where is your God?"

These things I remember, and I pour out my soul within me. For I used to go along with the throng and lead them in procession to the house of God, With the voice of joy and thanksgiving, a multitude keeping festival.

Why are you in despair, O my soul? And why have you become disturbed within me? Hope in God, for I shall again praise Him For the help of His presence. O my God, my soul is in despair within me; Therefore I remember Thee from the land of the Jordan, And the peaks of Hermon, from Mount Mizar.

Deep calls to deep at the sound of Thy waterfalls; All Thy breakers and Thy waves have rolled over me. The LORD will command His lovingkindness in the daytime; And His song will be with me in the night, A prayer to the God of my life.

I will say to God my rock, "Why hast Thou forgotten me? Why do I go mourning because of the oppression of the enemy?" As a shattering of my bones, my adversaries revile me, While they say to me all day long, "Where is your God?" Why are you in despair, O my soul? And why have you become disturbed within me? Hope in God, for I shall yet praise Him, The help of my countenance, and my God (Psalm 42:1-11).

Chapter 2

Understanding Seasons of Refreshing
Are You Thirsty?

Have you ever been thirsty? I mean really thirsty—not just thirsty enough to stop by at your favorite fast-food place for an ice cold Coke—but exhaustive in thirst. Like the Gator Aid commercials on television where one cannot consume the beverage fast enough to energize themselves. Similar to the runner on a marathon race who snatches a cup of water only to drink a little and pour the rest over his burning head, trying both to quench his thirst and cool himself down at the same time. Can you imagine what it would be like to run a marathon without having water available? The body would soon feel the effects of dehydration and be in serious trouble.

Dehydration occurs when there is a loss of water content and the essential body salts (electrolytes) needed for normal body functioning. There are basically three types of dehydration. Mild dehydration, which is said to set in when there is a fluid loss of 5% from the body. At this point in time, dehydration is not very dangerous and can be easily cured. Moderate dehydration is said to set in when there is up to a 10% loss of body fluid. This type is of great concern and immediate steps should be taken for re-hydration. When about 15% of a person's body fluid is lost, a person is considered severely dehydrated. This becomes a medical emergency and may require hospitalization to bring about a normal electrolyte balance. A person suffering from dehydration will display the following symptoms:

- Fatigue
- Dizziness, confusion, and coma
- Low blood pressure
- Severe thirst
- Increased heart rate and breathing, etc. (1)

Just as the runner experiences dehydration from lack of water, so do the crops when there is a lack of rain and drought conditions set in. Droughts can be devastating with the loss of food crops, livestock can be decimated, and the top soil can literally be carried away like the dust bowl in the early 1930's. Drought can affect the economy with high food prices, short supplies and poor quality. Droughts are also killers, as seen in the effects in East Africa.

Our soul is often like the runner who experiences dehydration or the crops of the land in a severe drought. When we continually pour ourselves out without taking any spiritual nourishment in, we become withered and dried up and like the ground, we become lifeless. A runner will often exert himself to the point where he cannot go on, it is called "hitting the wall." I have been told at this point, physical cramps set in, shortness of breath, fatigue, and extreme exhaustion where it becomes impossible to even walk. I have met many believers who are like that, as they have pushed themselves to the extreme where they simply cannot go on. They have experienced the "dehydration" of the soul; they have not taken anything in to quench their spiritual thirst. Like the phases of dehydration, the more they pour themselves out and not replenish themselves spiritually, the greater the chance for "burn out." Are you spiritually dehydrated, depleted of all the life-giving resources of the "living water?" Like the symptoms of dehydration, so too there are symptoms of spiritual dehydration. Here are a few to consider:

- Prayerlessness
- Lack of desire to study God's Word
- Powerlessness in resisting temptations
- A feeling of emptiness
- Spiritual fatigue
- A hardness of heart

The symptoms of spiritual dehydration can leave one void of the joy God intended for His children to have. The healing for spiritual dehydration can only be found in returning to an intimate relationship with Jesus Christ. Are you thirsty for Him? Only Jesus Christ can "re-hydrate" or fill us again with His "living water." Only He can quench your spiritual thirst completely. Jesus said to the woman at the well, *"Whoever drinks of the water that I shall give him shall never thirst: but the water that I shall give him shall become in him a well of water springing up to eternal life."* (3) She too, was thirsting for someone or something to satisfy the longing in her heart and found it in the person of Jesus Christ, never to "thirst" again. Many are longing to be re-hydrated, filled again with His living water, and this is "understanding" what seasons of refreshing is about.

Psalm 42 is a Psalm that will give us a look into a heart, which cries for God. This Psalm was probably a song or more likely a lamentation because it speaks of a heart's longing to be back in the presence of God. The Psalmist who wrote this was probably in exile, possibly David fleeing from Saul's persecution or Absalom's rebellion. If we draw the applications to ourselves, we too can be in exile, alone and apart from God because of sin. In desperation, we begin to develop a thirst for the living God and desire to return to His fellowship. We long to be satisfied with the living water that only He can provide. When we become thirsty—really thirsty—thirsting to the point of anguish like the runner suffering from dehydration, then we begin to understand the meaning of seasons of refreshing.

Longing for the Living God: (vs. 1-4)

"As the deer pants for the water brooks, So my soul pants for Thee, O God. My soul thirsts for God, for the living God; When shall I come and appear before God? My tears have

been my food day and night, While they say to me all day long, "Where is your God?" These things I remember, and I pour out my soul within me. For I used to go along with the throng and lead them in procession to the house of God, With the voice of joy and thanksgiving, a multitude keeping festival."

I. The Panting:

"As the deer pants for the water brooks."

Picture a deer running through the forest, fleeing from wolves. With all of her strength she runs, knowing if she stops disaster awaits. She is panting heavily, gasping for air, which is a sure sign of physical distress. She has an intense need to satisfy the thirst burning within her. She is looking desperately for the fresh water streams that so often run through the forests and once found she will drink long and deep to satisfy her need.

I have seen deer at streams drinking even though danger is about, as their need for water far out ways the desire for safety or shelter. The deer in this Psalm is panting for water, not greener leaves, a safer haven, or better shelters. In our case, it could be for newer cars, better jobs, bigger houses, friends that are more influential, greater income, etc. Water is what's needed most and she is desperate for it. That is her focus, desire, and need and she will not turn away until she finds it. She knows only water can satisfy her thirst and therefore she longs for its refreshing qualities.

"My soul pants for Thee, O God."

In the same characteristics as the deer, we can be running to the point of exhaustion and in need of "living water." *"My soul pants for Thee,"* the Psalmist was pushed to the limits, tired and exhausted, longing for the presence of God. It is this longing for intimacy with God that draws us closer to Him in order to be refreshed and renewed in His love. This sheer longing for seasons of refreshing in our lives is to take away the emptiness and frustrations of life. The panting often speaks of exasperation as we are at the end of our strength, and our only hope is in God. It is when we come to the end of "ourselves" that we realize how desperately we need "Him" in our lives.

The Psalmist was panting for God, not ease, comfort, position, or strength but communion with God was the urgency of his soul. The Psalmist realized how desperate he was for God and his heart cried out to Him. Matthew Henry's Commentary provides the following insight, *"Sometimes God teaches us to effectually know the worth of His mercies by the want of them, and whets our appetite for the means of grace by cutting us short on those means. We are more apt to despise the manna, when we have plenty of it, which will be very precious to us when we come to know the scarcity of it."* (4) It is when we are in want of His grace that we see how we need the LORD Jesus Christ in our lives. The Psalmist was deprived, in a great measure, of the inward comfort he used to have in God, and now he goes mourning and panting, longing to return.

> *Our panting, like the Psalmist, should be for God, not money, ease, power, or position, but for God alone.*

Our panting, like the Psalmist, should be for God, not money, ease, power, or position, but for God alone. Our longing should be to draw closer to Him and experience His presence in a deeper and more intimate way. We should be desperate for His communion, longing for His filling more than the necessity of water.

"My soul pants," his very self or his inner being, was crying out for God. Like the deer that brays for water, once found, is content and grateful. So the Psalmist prays to finds his LORD and once found is rejoicing and at peace. However, deny him his LORD, and his heart heaves, his bosom palpitates, his whole frame is convulsed, like the deer who gasps for breath, or the runner who pants after a marathon.

II. The Thirsting:

"My soul thirsts for God."

"My soul," all of my being or with all my heart, *"thirsts"*, or craves for, desires, is insatiable, *"for God."* What does it mean to thirst for God? It is to long for His presence, to commune with the Holy Spirit, and to experience again His peace within our lives. It is to desire God more than the necessities of life.

Just as one cannot live without water, we cannot live without the presence of God in our lives. Thirsting for God means desiring His Word, to read, study, and meditate on scriptures.

> *Thirsting for God is a longing to be used by Him no matter what the personal cost may be or where He may lead.*

Jeremiah, the Prophet said, *"Thy words were found, and I did eat them; and thy word was unto me the joy and rejoicing of mine heart."* (5)

Devouring scriptures as the Holy Spirit directs, brings a deep satisfaction to the soul as we hunger to know and fellowship with Him. Thirsting for God is a longing to be used by Him no matter what the personal cost may be or where He may lead. Our thirst is to do His will and our panting is to seek His approval.

Similar to these verses is Psalm 63:1 David states, *"O God, thou art my God; early will I seek thee: my soul thirsteth for thee, my flesh longeth for thee in a dry and thirsty land, where no water is"* (KJV). My soul *"thirsts"* and my flesh *"longs,"* is the consuming desire of a heart that cries for God. There is a sense of anguish or pain involved in the need for or a longing to have a deeper relationship with God. Just as we long for home and our families after an extensive time of travel, so too, is our desire to be home with our Savior and LORD. There is the pain of separation and the intense longing to be in fellowship and communion with the One who loves us supremely.

"For the living God."

The Psalmist was longing for the *"living God,"* not materialism, wealth, position or status. These too often become the "gods" we long for and leave us thirsting for something more. No, it is the living God that is desired because only He cares about our every longing and promises to meet our every need. The focus of the Psalmist's cry was God, the *living God*, in opposition to dead idols as works of man's hands. He longed for the living God who alone can open up the fountains of living water and quench the thirst of the needy, satisfying the barrenness of the soul. It is the living God that we also long for and are desperate to fellowship with. Many times, we have gone after the broken down idols of this world. These idols of materialism have left us dry and desolate. The idols of wealth and power have left us empty and barren, and the idols of prestige and status have left us hardened and lifeless. The living God, as opposed to the dead and meaningless idols, is our longing and our panting.

"When shall I appear before God?"

As the soul thirsts for God, there is a longing to return to times of worship. Worship is a part of thirsting for God, as we desire to lift Him up in praise and thanksgiving for all He is and has done. Worship comes from a heart filled with love and adoration for God, as we acknowledge His Lordship over our lives. The Psalmist David said to, *"Give unto the LORD the glory due unto His name; worship the LORD in the beauty of holiness."* (6) To give unto the LORD the glory due His name means He alone is worthy of worship

> *In summary, the panting is the longing and wanting of the soul's deep need for communion with God.*

and praise. He alone is holy in all that He is and does. The Psalmist asked, "when," for there was the desire and need to be in God's presence again to worship and adore Him. The Psalmist longed to be in God's presence and so should we.

In summary, the panting is the longing and wanting of the soul's deep need for communion with God. It is the desire to fellowship with God on an intimate basis more than life itself. The thirsting for God is the desire and the need to worship. When we have a heart ready to worship and wanting to praise and magnify the name of Jesus, to seek Him with all of our being, we are beginning to understand seasons of refreshing. But a part of the panting and thirsting are the tears, for they speak of a broken heart and David said, *"A broken heart and a contrite heart, O God, Thou will not despise"* (Ps 51:17).

III.   The Tears:

"My tears have been my food day and night."

Tears are healthful to the soul. When a person comes to tears, they are earnest and sincere in their longing.   The

Psalmist's food was his tears—there wasn't an appetite for anything else. He had no joy or reason for rejoicing, just tears and lots of them. He was broken over two things, and if we have a heart that cries for God, we too are broken. First, God was being blasphemed. *"While they say to me, where is your God?"* These are the cruel mocking of misguided men who think God either doesn't exist, He is uncaring, uninvolved, or unaware of the circumstance the Psalmist, or we are in. We too should be broken, as the Psalmist was, over the cruel taunting of wicked men who blaspheme God continually. Their mocking of *"where is your God,"* is implied to make us doubt and question God's love and promises. However, God is near to those who call upon Him and He is faithful to His Word. Secondly, the Psalmist was in tears because he longed for the times of worship in the house of God: times of joy and thanksgiving when songs of praise to the One who is worthy were sung. This brought tears to the Psalmist eyes as he remembered those times. Do we miss our times of fellowship with the LORD in the same way? The Psalmist wept because he longed to worship in the house (temple) of God, do we have the same desire for our house of worship? The tears shed are not only for blaspheme of God, but for the anguish to fellowship with other believers in the LORD's house.

The Psalmist, when he reflected on this, poured out his soul. We too remember former times of worship and fellowship with other believers. We remember precious moments of drawing close to the Savior during times of trouble and finding His grace sufficient for our every need. Are there tears from cutting yourselves off from God's blessings? Is there a longing to return to an intimate relationship with Him? This is what panting and thirsting for God is about. God is a heart's cry away and desires to renew the fellowship we once experienced. God said through Jeremiah, the prophet, *"And you shall seek Me and find Me, when you search for Me with all your heart. And I will be found by you."* (7) If you are panting and thirsting for God to the point of tears take courage, God has promised He will be found by you.

The Psalmist's tears were a result of brokenness and sorrow over unbelievers mocking God. If we have a heart that pants and thirst for God, it will grieve us as well. It will anger us when His Word is denied, scorned or ridiculed, and it will humble us when we think how we were like that until His grace found us. Are there tears when we hear God's name mocked? Part of understanding seasons of refreshing, is to be burdened for the holiness of God.

Understanding personal revival is longing for the living God, but it also involves learning from the living God. The times of thirsting, panting, and the tears are a part of growing in the knowledge and fellowship of our LORD. Times of despair, anguish, and loneliness are often allowed by Him in order to bring us back into His presence that we may experience His grace and mercy.

Learning from the Living God:

Psalm 42:5-11

"Why are you in despair, O my soul? And why have you become disturbed within me? Hope in God, for I shall again praise Him For the help of His presence. O my God, my soul is in despair within me; Therefore I remember Thee from the land of the Jordan, And the peaks of Hermon, from Mount Mizar. Deep calls to deep at the sound of Thy waterfalls; All Thy breakers and Thy waves have rolled over me."

"The LORD will command His lovingkindness in the daytime; And His song will be with me in the night, A prayer to the God of my life. I will say to God my rock, "Why hast Thou forgotten me? Why do I go mourning because of the oppression of the enemy?" As a shattering of my bones, my adversaries revile me, While they say to me all day long, "Where is your God?" Why are you in despair, O my soul? And why have you become disturbed within me? Hope in God, for I shall yet praise Him, The help of my countenance, and my God."

I. Hope in God.

"Why are you in despair, O my soul? And why have you become disturbed within me? Hope in God, for I shall again praise Him For the help of His presence."

When we pant and thirst for God, broken to the point of tears, God will answer our cry. We will again experience His presence and power within us. The question the Psalmist asked, *"Why are you in despair, O my soul,"* could be answered by the following phrase. *"Hope in God,"* for God is unchangeable, and therefore His grace is our grounds for this unshakeable hope. It does not matter how dark the night or how deep the waters, our

Heavenly Father is our help and He will never forsake us. *"Hope in God,"* is to have confidence in His Word and to trust Him completely. We are commanded to be strong in faith because He is all-powerful, all knowing, and ever-present. He is the One who is the same yesterday, today, and forever and the One who is sovereign, who sees the end from the beginning. That is our hope!

Sometimes it takes times of despair, trials, setbacks, maybe sickness, or a loss of a loved one for us to realize how desperately we need God. The Psalmist was in despair in his exile, as if the waters of doom and gloom were drowning him. He states, *"All Thy breakers and Thy waves have rolled over me,"* as he was being swept away by discouragement and despair. His lighthouse of hope was in God, for He was there to rescue him and He is there for us. Learning from the living God lesson one: during times of despair, hope in God, for He alone can deliver us and He alone is our hope.

II. Rest in God.

"The LORD will command His lovingkindness in the daytime; And His song will be with me in the night, A prayer to the God of my life."

After every storm, the calm is restored. The Psalmist spoke of the breakers and waves that had rolled over on him (v. 7). Like a fishing boat in a hurricane, they are caught in the midst of a storm and there is no way out. This is similar to the Disciples, as they rowed their tiny boat in the midst of a sever storm. Helpless against the elements, and when all seemed hopeless, they cried out to Jesus for help, and He rebuked the winds with the words, *"Peace, be still."* (8) As One having the authority, the winds and the waves instantly obeyed Him. *He commands His loving-kindness toward us,* and like the winds and waves, mercy and grace are instantly given to His chosen. No day shall ever dawn that God's love shall not rain down on His elect. God's loving-kindness will always be there in the morning even though the night is filled with sorrow. David said, *"weeping may endure for the night, but joy cometh in the morning."* (9) We can have rest in the midst of any storm knowing God's loving-kindness is directed toward us.

"His song will be with me in the night."

Songs of praise and worship shall encourage the faint-hearted in the night. When the gloom of darkness has set in, and hope has begun to wane, He is our song bringing forth light. Whatever fears we may face, or trials we may endure, He is our hope and our rejoicing. The night, at times, can be very lonely and empty, but we can fill it with songs of praise as we worship Him. The darkness of the night cannot put out His light of hope. His light illuminates every shadow and turns the darkness of the night into the brightness of a noonday. *His song is a song of hope and praise, a song of triumphant and victory,* and a song of love and redemption. That song is in our hearts through the darkest of nights and the brightest of days.

Learning from the living God lesson two; rest in God. He will surround us with His loving-kindness and fill us with a song in the night seasons.

III.   Wait on God.

"Hope in God, for I shall yet praise Him, The help of my countenance, and my God."

Learning from the living God also involves waiting on Him. The Psalmist states, *"for I shall yet praise Him,"* he was looking for deliverance to come and he would erupt into praise when it happened. His complaint was his enemies have oppressed and reproached him and he went about mourning day to day and from place to place (v. 9). His comfort is the fact that God is his *rock* (v. 9)—a rock to build upon and to take shelter in. To the Psalmist and to us, we have access—with confidence unto God our rock. Therefore, we can say with assurance, *we do not have to be cast down, O my soul!* Learning from the living God lesson three: wait on God, for He is our help and our strength, and will deliver us.

Hope in God, rest in God, and wait on God these are the lessons to learn from the living God. In times of despair, He is our hope, our confidence, and the One in whom we have placed our faith. In times of troubles, He is our rest, the One who will encourage us with His love, show us His mercy, and give grace to help in time of need. In times of persecution and trials, He is our deliverer as we wait upon Him, for He is our help and our God.

Application:

Understanding seasons of refreshing involves two criteria. First, it begins when we long for the living God. At the beginning of the chapter the question was asked, "Are you thirsty?" To understand seasons of refreshing is to have a spiritual thirst only God can satisfy. Longing for the living God involves the panting of the soul to be in God's presence again. It creates a thirsting for God that only He can fill. It involves tears because there is a deep longing for God that produces brokenness within.

Understanding seasons of refreshing involves secondly, learning from the living God. In times of despair, we are to hope in God for He alone can bring us through the difficulties we face. It also means to rest in God. Though the world is uncertain and full of discouragement and trials, we can rest in Him for He has commanded His loving-kindness toward us. It will mean to wait on God, even when facing persecution and sufferings, for He is our rock and the foundation of our hope. We can have confidence in our God and praise Him for His deliverance. The panting for God will produce hope, for He will sustain us. The thirsting for God will produce rest, as He will satisfy the longings of our heart. And the tears will produce patience, as we wait on God, our strength and our deliverer. Are you thirsty for God? Is there a deep longing for God's presence in your life? If we do not pant or thirst for Jesus Christ in our life, we cannot experience the seasons of refreshing that God has promised us. This refreshing will only come when we are willing to repent and return to Him. Acts 3:19 states, *"Repent therefore and return, that your sins may be wiped away, in order that times of refreshing may come from the presence of the LORD."* Repent and return is the cry to come back to God with hearts longing for His presence and a willingness to learn from His leading. He then will shower on us times (seasons) of refreshing from His presence. When we long for Him, He will fill us with the Holy Spirit afresh and anew.

Let this prayer be the cry of your heart.

"Father, as the deer panteth for the water brocks so my soul longs for Thee. You alone are my heart's desire, my longing, my strength, and the hope of my salvation. O precious Father, draw me near to Thee and fill me with Thy Holy Spirit. Break me of my pride and my desires until Your will becomes my longing and Your heart becomes my fire. Father, I have tasted of this world and found it to be bitter. Now, renew my heart and send revival to my soul. In Jesus name, Amen."

Recall & Application

1. What does it mean to "pant after God?"

_____

_____

_____

2. Describe what it means to "thirst after God" in your life?

_____

_____

_____

3. Learning from the living God involved what three things?

_____

_____

_____

4. In what areas are you experiencing the "dehydration of the soul?"

_____

_____

_____

5. When God is "blasphemed," what is your reaction?

_____

_____

_____

6. When God speaks, do I listen? God spoke to me in the following ways:

_____

_____

And Elijah came near to all the people and said, "How long will you hesitate between two opinions? If the LORD is God, follow Him; but if Baal, follow him." But the people did not answer him a word.

Then Elijah said to all the people, "Come near to me." So all the people came near to him. And he repaired the altar of the LORD, which had been torn down. And Elijah took twelve stones according to the number of the tribes of the sons of Jacob, to whom the word of the LORD had come, saying, "Israel shall be your name." So with the stones he built an altar in the name of the LORD, and he made a trench around the altar, large enough to hold two measures of seed.

Then he arranged the wood and cut the ox in pieces and laid it on the wood. And he said, "Fill four pitchers with water and pour it on the burnt offering and on the wood."
And he said, "Do it a second time," and they did it a second time. And he said, "Do it a third time," and they did it a third time. And the water flowed around the altar, and he also filled the trench with water.

Then it came about at the time of the offering of the evening sacrifice, that Elijah the prophet came near and said, "O LORD, the God of Abraham, Isaac and Israel, today let it be known that Thou art God in Israel, and that I am Thy servant, and that I have done all these things at Thy word. "Answer me, O LORD, answer me, that this people may know that Thou, O LORD, art God, and that Thou hast turned their heart back again."

Then the fire of the LORD fell, and consumed the burnt offering and the wood and the stones and the dust, and licked up the water that was in the trench. And when all the people saw it, they fell on their faces; and they said, "The LORD, He is God; the LORD, He is God."
(One kings 18:21; 30-39)

Chapter 3

Conditions for Seasons of Refreshing.
Do You Want to See the Fire?

Have you ever seen a forest fire? Have you ever seen the raging flames engulfing thousands of acres destroying everything in its path leaving only devastation behind? The billowing smoke from the raging inferno can be seen from miles away. Sometimes the smoke from a forest fire can settle over a town and literally block out the sun. The causes of forest fires can vary from the most common, lightning, to the carelessness of an unattended campfire. Once started, they can be devastating to everything in its path and sometimes they will burn until the winter snows finally extinguish them. During the summer of 1988, there were 13 different fires raging in Yellowstone National Park. The combination of high winds, hot weather, and drought conditions produced one of the worst fires in history. Before the September snows finally quenched the blazes, over one million acres had been burned. (1) In the late summer of 2000, bush fires were raging across 11 states with nearly 60,000 fires reported at one time destroying over 4 million acres. Nearly 21,000 firefighters were deployed, as they fought the worst outbreak in bush fires in 50 years. (2) The effects of a forest fire are devastating often leaving the ground barren of life, taking decades before a thriving forest is growing again.

When we think of a forest fire, there are three main characteristics that each fire possesses. First, a forest fire will consume everything in its path. The raging fire with its intense heat literally devours the landscape leaving only charred remains. Second, a forest fire will cleanse the land. The consuming fire will burn all the underbrush along with the dead and decaying trees that have fallen, cleansing the land of all that is diseased and dying. Third, a forest fire will change the landscape, often times permanently. These characteristics of forest fires can be applied to the conditions for seasons of refreshing, case in point—the prophet Elijah.

The Desperation of a Prophet.

We know little about Elijah's past or his occupation. Yet, his name meant *"Yahweh is my God,"* and during times of idolatry and rebellion towards the true God, His name alone would produce confrontation. Perhaps it was seeing his nation move from the worship of "Yahweh" to serving a foreign god known as Baal that broke his heart. Maybe he realized God in His Holiness could not continue to look the other way while His people participated in open sin. Either way, he was burdened and broken for the things that broke God's heart. In understanding Elijah's heart and the need for revival, we must first look at the past sins of his nations that led to the present judgments.

I. Past Sins: (1 Kings 16:29-34)

Ahab was now King of Israel and the commentary on his life was, *"And Ahab the son of Omri, did evil in the sight of the LORD more than all who were before him."* (3) Ahab was a wicked, self-seeking king, who married a women more evil than himself. Together they brought idol worship into the land for all to serve, and they did it in such a manner, which far exceeded all the wickedness of the previous kings. Jezebel was Ahab's Queen and she was a wicked and domineering woman who became the vassal King. She had enticed Ahab to build a temple in honor of Baal that contained his image for all to worship. History records the ritual of Baal worship involved all kinds of perverse sexual practices, in order to invoke his blessings. All this was done in mockery to the LORD God and His commandments, which they choose to ignore and disobey. Summing it up, scripture records, *"Ahab did more to provoke the LORD God than all the kings of Israel before him"* (1 Kings 16:33). Because of Ahab and his wife Jezebel, the occult practice known as Baal worship led the entire kingdom into idolatry, sexual immorality, perversion, blood shedding and blaspheme of God. God then brought judgment upon the nation in order to awaken and return them to His commandments.

Israel's past is our present. We, as a nation, have become steeped in idolatry, sexual immorality, perversion, blood shedding, and blaspheme of God. Have the sins of the world become the sins of the church? Is there idolatry, sexual immorality, perversion and open blaspheme of God among God's people? Sadly, there is and scriptures are clear in warning, Paul states, *"But do not let immorality or any impurity or greed even be named among you, as is proper among saints."* (4) In other words, these sins should not be mentioned as part of our conduct since the blood of Christ has delivered us. To continue in these sins without repentance, leaves a question of being genuinely born again! Note what Paul said, *"For this you know with certainty, that no immoral or impure person or covetous man, who is an idolater, has an inheritance in the kingdom of Christ and God."* (5) Blunt and to the point! If we really desire personal revival, a fresh filling of His presence, and a renewed intimacy with Him, these sins, whether past or present—need to be repented of.

II. Present Judgments: (1 Kings 17:1)

> *The effects of droughts are devastating. But when a drought lasts for three and half years, you have a catastrophe in epic proportions.*

The effects of droughts are devastating. However, when a drought lasts for three and half years, you have a catastrophe in epic proportions. This was Elijah's announcement to the people; neither dew nor rain would come until God would give the command. One can imagine what the effects would be on the land, the economy, and the people of that day. Not only would they have lost their first years crops, but also the rains would not be there for the winter crops, etc. Soon the land would become desolate of life, barren, and dusty. The winds would literally blow the topsoil right off in blinding dust storms. The effects on livestock would be disastrous. Many would die and those left would be weak and sickly from malnutrition. Whole herds would be wiped out, and if some could be spared and protected from the elements, the cost of maintaining them would be astronomical. Eventually, every person would feel the effects of the drought conditions. Raising food prices would begin to escalate and water wells would begin to dry up. Starvation would start taking its toll and many would die. Malnutrition would be a common sight among the poor and less fortunate; disease would run ramped throughout the communities. Water would be the scarcest of commodities and selling for a premium price, probably exceeding the value of gold and silver of that day. Everywhere one would look, there would be the effects of the drought: cracked and barren land with diseased and dying livestock, and worst of all, malnourished children. The economy would be in shambles, and even the King in his royal chambers would suffer want.

There would be no escaping the effects of this drought, God would see to that.

Present judgments are wake up calls to a nation that has ignored God, even though He has provided and protected them for years. It is an alarm clock to believers to return to prayer and repentance; God is speaking and His voice is getting louder! In was a drought in Israel's case, in our case, it could be a natural disaster or even a terrorist attack. It is not that God is singling out individuals for His wrath. Rather, it is a corporate plea to return and seek mercy and forgiveness. Israel did not and the drought lasted for three and a half years!

Putting the pieces together, you can see the conditions Elijah faced when returning to Mount Carmel. The people were desperate, the situation was critical, and the conditions were right for God to do a miracle. Just like today, God is still in the miracle working business.

Israel's Question: (our question) (1 Kings 18:21)

And Elijah came near to all the people and said, "How long will you hesitate between two opinions? If the LORD is God, follow Him; but if Baal, follow him." But the people did not answer him a word.

This is a tragic question with an even greater tragic result, silence! Think of the devastation, the loss of life, the suffering of the people, and yet when asked to make a choice, they cannot or will not. It is called "riding the fence" or "wanting the best from both worlds" and it will not work. However, before we get to critical of the people in Elijah's day, let us look at the idols present within Christianity today.

"Idol worship," we may not make an image out of wood or clay to bow down to and we probably do not even give idol worship much thought. After all, we are too sophisticated, and besides, that kind of practice takes place among "those heathen jungle people." Right? However, a good definition of an idol is anything or anyone taking the place of God in ones life. An idol can be job or a career, it can be a favorite "sin" constantly repeated or committed. Money can be an idol when we hoard it, covet it, and will do anything to gain it. People can become idols, and if you are in doubt on this one, look at your average rock star or sports hero! Things we covet become idols, because they control our mind, emotions, and will. We really do not have to go to Africa to find idols, because they are within us. Remember the first commandment, *"You shall have no gods before Me."* (6) We may not bow down to worship "other gods" but we will pay homage to the gods of this world. Money, possessions, status, all becomes the gods we serve in order to become what society calls successful.

Elijah challenged the people to a confrontation on who was the true God. They were to set up a sacrifice and call upon Baal; in return, Elijah would set up a sacrifice and call upon the LORD. The "god" who answered by fire would be God. This would be a tremendous challenge, placing the God who is, against the "gods" who are not! The people labored intently, calling out to Baal and finally cutting themselves as a blood offering to him—a god who does not see, hear, or care about their suffering or their needs. Are we really any different today? The gods we often serve are just as cold and indifferent, and at the end of the day, they like most of us, are tired, burned out, broken and bleeding trying to please the "gods' who are not instead of seeking the God who is. It is in this emptiness and frustration that we are about to understand the conditions for seasons of refreshing.

Elijah knew God must do something supernatural to bring this people back to Him. When they reached the "end of themselves," Elijah was ready to demonstrate the power of the living LORD. The true God would be the one who answered by fire but before this could happen; Elijah had to rebuild the altar, arrange the wood, and offer the sacrifice. Each one of these parts has a special meaning for those who long to see God move in our lives. However, if we are to meet the conditions for seasons of refreshing, we must first answer the question, "Do you want to see the fire?"

The Altar, the Wood, and the Sacrifice.

Then Elijah said to all the people, "Come near to me." So all the people came near to him. And he repaired the altar of the LORD, which had been torn down. And Elijah took twelve stones according to the number of the tribes of the sons of

60

Jacob, to whom the word of the LORD had come, saying, "Israel shall be your name." So with the stones he built an altar in the name of the LORD. (1 Kings 18:30-33)

I. The Altar:

Before the fire of God would consume the sacrifice, the altar needed to be repaired. Elijah began by repairing the broken down altar once dedicated to the LORD; he would not use one polluted by the priests of Baal. The altar had been neglected for

> *We have heard thousands of sermons on revival and attended conferences by the dozens and yet, revival still hasn't come. The reason—we are quite content to live without it.*

years, along with the sacrifice of worship and offerings of praise. In this case, the altar was torn down as an attempt to rid the countryside of any memory of the LORD God who they once served. After all, if there were not an altar there would be no remembrance of God or His commandments and, therefore, no conviction of sin. Right? Wrong! Even when we try to banish God from our thoughts, He is there to bring conviction for our sin—leading us to repentance.

We, as a nation, can remove the Ten Commandments from our public places, we can banish prayer in our classrooms, and we can remove nativity scenes, however, that will not stop the haunting emptiness coming from a life without Jesus Christ.

"Elijah repaired the altar of the LORD," note that he did not build a new one. His desire was not to introduce a new religion, program, self-help therapy, positive thinking seminar, or any other psychobabble of the day. His desire was revival, to see them return to the God of their fathers, to restore their first love. Revival was what they needed and so do we. We have had an abundance of self-help seminars put on by entertainers rather than genuine ministers of God. We have heard thousands of sermons on revival and attended conferences by the dozens and yet, revival still has not come. The reason—we are quite content to live without it. The "feel good" seminars of the day accomplish just that, they make one feel good! In reality, what is needed is the crying out for mercy and forgiveness. The laughter and entertainment at these seminars needs to be replaced with weeping and lamentation for our offenses to a holy God.

When we begin to repair the altars, we can see the need for personal revival—a returning to our first love. Jesus would later say to the church at Ephesus, *"But I have this against you, that you have left your first love. Remember therefore from where you have fallen, and repent and do the deeds you did at first; or else I am coming to you, and will remove your lampstand out of its place - unless you repent."* (8) The church at Ephesus would loose their lampstand, the light of their testimony, if they would not repent and return to their first love. They needed to rebuild the altars that had been torn down.

Altars were used as a place for sacrifice, needed to approach God. Jesus has become our sacrifice; His blood has made atonement for our sin once and for all. However, are there altars needing repaired in your life? If altars represent places of sacrifice, then here are a few suggestions of altars that may need to be repaired:

- Time of repentance and self-examination.
- Time for Bible study and devotions.
- Time spent in fasting and prayer.
- Commitment to holy living.
- Having a right relationship with others.
- Giving of time and finances.
- Serving and using the spiritual gifts that God has entrusted to you.

These are altars that may need to be repaired in your life in order to see the fire of God fall. So Elijah repaired the altar *in the name of the LORD*, that is, by His direction and for His glory.

II. The Wood:

"Then he arranged the wood and cut the ox in pieces and laid it on the wood. And he said, "Fill four pitchers with water and pour it on the burnt offering and on the wood." And he said, "Do it a second time," and they did it a second time. And he said, "Do it a third time," and they did it a third time. And the water flowed around the altar, and he also filled the trench with water." (1 Kings 18:33-35)

Every fire needs a source of fuel. In order for wood to be a source, it must meet three conditions. First, it needs to be seasoned or dried out so it will burn. Second, it needs to be conducive for burning. And third, the wood needs to be broken in pieces in order to burn thoroughly. After the altar was repaired, the wood had to be found and made ready. In order for the sacrifice to completely burn, the right amount of kindling would be mixed in with the seasoned wood. But in this case, water was poured repeatedly on the wood until it was completely soaked and entirely unable to ignite. This, however, instead of becoming a hindrance to the power of God actually enhanced it. This wood would now be sufficient fuel for the fire of God. What seems impossible in man's eyes was and is probable with God.

If God is to consume us with His fire, we too must be as the wood used in burning the sacrifice. First, we need to be seasoned; sin, like the moisture in wood, must be removed. Second, we must be conducive for

> *We must be broken, as branches are snapped and used for kindling; we too must be stripped of pride and self—ready for the Master's use.*

His fire, which is a willingness to be used by and for Him. Third, we must be broken, as branches are snapped and used for kindling; we too must be stripped of pride and self—ready for the Master's use.

III.   The Sacrifice:

"Elijah cut the ox in pieces and laid it on the wood." Elijah would have remembered the commands of the LORD on how the sacrifice must be prepared and those customs would have been observed. To fully understand the importance of the offering of the sacrifice, let us look at God's requirements for the burnt offering found in Leviticus chapter one. The sacrifice must be:

(A) Without Defect. = (Lev 1:3)

That is without spot or blemish. It could not be sick or lame, and it was to be a male, the very best of the flock. Would God demand anything less? It was to be perfect in honor of the One who was infinitely perfect in all that He is. If we are to present ourselves as living sacrifices, we must be clean from the defect of sin and only the blood of Jesus Christ can do that. The priest would examine the sacrifice before it was offered, for they knew God would reject it if did not meet this requirement. Later in Israel's history, the book of Malachi would warn the people about offering up that which was lame and blind. So sickly were the animals used, God responded by calling it evil and asking if they would dare to offer this to their governor, and if so, would he be pleased with what is set before him (Malachi 1:8)?

God would call it useless fire, a waste of time, because He was not pleased with their offering. If we are to present ourselves as living sacrifices, without defect, shouldn't we seek cleansing and forgiveness also?

(B) It had to be Accepted. = (Lev 1:4)

The owner was to offer the sacrifice with a willing heart, full of love and repentance to God. The owner himself would lay his hands on the head of the animal as a sign of acceptance to make atonement on his behalf. Though the burnt offering did not point to any particular sin; they were to make atonement for sin in general. As the owner laid his hands on the head of the burnt offering, he was to confess his guilt of sin and disobedience. He was also to pray that though he deserved to die himself, the death of this sacrifice might be accepted for the expiating of his guilt.

(C) The Blood had to be Applied. = (Lev 1:5)

After the bullock was killed, the priest would take the blood and sprinkle it around the altar. One could not approach God without the shedding of innocent blood. It was the blood that made atonement for the soul. And it is the blood of Jesus Christ, which has to be applied to our lives for us to be cleansed from sin. He is our atonement—the perfect sacrifice. The Apostle Peter stated that it is the applying of the blood of our LORD Jesus Christ, by faith, that signified the pacifying and purifying of our conscience (1 Peter 1:2). The blood "applied" brought forgiveness of sin and satisfied the Father's justice—restoring fellowship with Him.

(D) The Flesh had to be removed. = (Lev 1:6)

Next, the priest would remove the flesh or skin of the bullock, for it would be contaminated and unclean. The sacrifice would not be accepted with the flesh still on. In the flesh, we cannot serve or please God. Just as the flesh was removed in order for the sacrifice to be pleasing to God, so our flesh must be stripped away. Paul would later say in the Epistle to the Romans, that nothing good dwells in the flesh, and they who are in the flesh, cannot please God (Romans 8:8). This means anything done in the flesh, no matter how good it may be in our own eyes, is hostile toward God! Note that the flesh was not cleaned or washed but removed. It is not man's efforts that gain acceptance to God, but their removal. When the flesh is removed, the spirit is exposed, ready to be consumed by the fire of God.

(E) The Bullock would be cut into Pieces. (Lev 1:6)

The priest would carefully and methodically cut the bullock into segments and arrange them on the altar. The knife would gracefully find the division in the joints and separate the primal pieces, leaving nothing untouched by it. It was as if the knife was searching for anything that might be hidden and needed to be brought to the light. So too, must God's holy knife cut through our hearts exposing anything hidden before Him. The writer of the book of Hebrews stated, *"For the word of God is living and active and sharper than any two-edged sword, and piercing as far as the division of soul and spirit, of both joints and marrow, and able to judge the thoughts and intentions of the heart."* (9) Like the bullock cut into pieces leaving nothing unexposed, so too God must search our hearts bringing to light what needs to be confessed and forsaken. The hidden idols of the heart must be exposed and cast out if we, the sacrifice, are to be accepted. If we are to meet the conditions for seasons of refreshing, personal revival, nothing can be hidden from God. In Joshua chapter seven, Achan, after the conquest of Jericho, thought he could hide some of the treasures he had taken. Even though God had expressly forbid taking anything, Achan took "things," thinking he would never be found out. Yet, God knew and the end result cost the lives of his family and himself. (10) We are only deceiving ourselves when we try to hide what must be confessed before Him. We will never experience the fire of God in our lives if we hide sin. Therefore, we must be honest in our confession of sin and ask our loving Father to "cut it out" of our lives.

(F) Washed with Water. (Lev 1:9)

The Priest would then wash the pieces of the bullock to cleanse them from any contamination, which might have occurred. Likewise, as God's Word cuts through our hearts exposing sin and defilement, we need to be washed and cleansed. Like the old hymn whose chorus goes *"Are you washed in the blood, In the soul-cleansing blood of the Lamb? Are your garments spotless? Are they white as snow? Are you washed in the blood of the Lamb?"* (11) If there were any contamination in the sacrifice, God would not accept it. Therefore, the priest would thoroughly wash the pieces of the bullock, leaving nothing to chance.

Elijah had requested four pitchers of water to be filled three different times and poured over the offering. Maybe he did this as a symbol of the desperate need for the cleansing of his people; or to show that God is still in the miracle working business. Either way there was enough water poured out it was left standing in the trenches Elijah had dug around the altar. During times of severe drought, the most precious commodity and least available is water and Elijah had just asked for twelve large barrels full! I can imagine after each request to fill the barrels again, someone would comment, *"Does he know what he is asking for?"* Elijah did, because he wanted to see the fire fall. Do You?

Sometimes preparing a sacrifice involves sacrificing. Elijah proved this earlier with the widow at Zarephath when he asked her for a jar of water and a

> *Sometimes preparing a sacrifice involves sacrificing.*

piece of bread (1 Kings 17). Not much to ask for unless it is all you have. The widow was preparing the last measure of flour she had for her son and herself. She too, probably thought, "Does he know what he is asking?" Yet, Elijah would insist on her bringing the bread to him first. In doing so, God would allow the bowl to be full of flour and the jar filled with oil until the rains came again. (12) It was an act of faith that she presented her last meal to Elijah, as a sacrifice, and God blessed it for she had no lack as a result. Do you want to see the fire?

In another instance, Jesus was at the grave sight of His friend, Lazarus (John 11). The air was thick with the cries of mourners and the critics of the day, as Jesus had commanded Martha to roll away the stone blocking the entrance to the tomb. Martha's response too was, "Does He know what He is asking?" *"LORD, by this time there will be a stench, for he has been dead four days."* Jesus response, like Elijah's, *"Did I not say to you, if you believe, you will see the glory of God?"* (13) That day the glory of God was revealed, as Jesus raised His friend Lazarus from the grave. Do you want to see the fire? Are you willing to be the sacrifice?

The altar was repaired, the wood was arranged, and the sacrifice was offered. It was time then to start the fire, only this time it would be done by the one true God.

III. The Prayer:

"Then it came about at the time of the offering of the evening sacrifice, that Elijah the prophet came near and said, "O LORD, the God of Abraham, Isaac and Israel, today let it be known that Thou art God in Israel, and that I am Thy servant, and that I have done all these things at Thy word. "Answer me, O LORD, answer me, that this people may know that Thou, O LORD, art God, and that Thou hast turned their heart back again." Then the fire of the LORD fell, and consumed the burnt offering and the wood and the stones and the dust, and licked up the water that was in the trench." (1 Kings 18:36-38)

It really is a simple prayer to look at—containing just sixty-four words, but it was powerful enough to send down the fire of God. This short prayer offered publicly, was only after lengthy times in agonizing prayer alone with God. His appeal was for God's holiness and righteousness to be vindicated. Elijah asked two things in this prayer. First, that God's glory would be revealed, *"let it be known that Thou art God in Israel."* All the worship and the glory must go to the LORD God, for He only is true and worthy of worship. *"And that I am Thy servant, and that I have done all these things at Thy word."* All Elijah had done or would do was at God's beckoning and in accordance with His will. Elijah sought not his own vindication as a prophet, but that God would receive what is rightfully His, praise and honor. Secondly, he sought the revival of the people. *"That this people may know that Thou, O LORD, art God."* He was asking God to remove the blinders that the false idols had created and to give the people new eyes to behold God. *"And that Thou hast turned their heart back again."* Only God could break their hardened hearts and call them back to Himself. Elijah's appeal was for grace and mercy to be showered on them as He had done so many times before. *"Answer me, O LORD, answer me,"* was the cry of his heart, as he waited in anticipation for God to send down the fire.

When all the conditions had been met and in response to Elijah's prayer and faithfulness, God answered. *"Then the fire of the LORD fell."* The fire literally consumed the sacrifice, evaporated the water, and devoured the stones of the altar. But most importantly, it changed the people's hearts, for they began shouting, *"The LORD, He is God; the LORD, He is God."* The God who answered by fire, He is God!

Application:

In the beginning of this chapter, we talked about the characteristic of forest fires. Fire; consumes everything in its path, cleanses the land, and changes the landscape permanently. So too, the fire of God when it falls on us as the sacrifice, will consume everything. All we are, desire, or hope to be will be engulfed in His flame of righteousness. Secondly, His fire will burn away all the dross, sin, self, and devour the heart of stone within us. Leaving us, thirdly, changed never to be the same again. Do you want to see the fire? In order for us to experience the fire of God in our lives, let us take what we have learned from this story of Elijah and apply it to the conditions for seasons of refreshing.

Altars, as we have learned, represented a place of sacrifice, a place where one would present an offering as an act of worship to a Holy God. Repairing an altar is to rebuild or renew a place of commitment to the LORD. Maybe the first altar that needs to be repaired is time alone with God. Time spent in worship, prayer, and the study of God's Word, time to offer the sacrifice of praise unto Him for His faithfulness unto us. Other altars, which may need to be rebuilt, are altars of moral purity, altars of obedience and faithfulness, altars of right living and a holy character. Altars also represented a place of death, for it was where the sacrifice was prepared on. As we repair our altars, let us do so with the thought that on the altar I must be willing to die to self. The conditions for seasons of refreshing demand that altars once again, be repaired and established. Do you want to see the fire?

The wood represented fuel for the fire. If we are to experience God's fire within us, we must become His fuel. The fuel God is looking for is a clean life, a life washed by the blood of Christ and made pure. A life that has nothing hidden, like the bullock cut into pieces and washed, we too are exposed before Him and cleansed. All idols are removed; anything that takes the place of Christ's preeminence in our life is destroyed. He alone becomes the God we serve and love. *"For the eyes of the LORD run to and fro throughout the whole earth, to show himself strong in the behalf of them whose heart is perfect toward him."* (14) God is looking for a heart perfect toward Him, a heart clean and ready to be used by Him. A heart, which longs for His presence and power in their life, and one who is surrendered and yielded to God's leading. This is a heart that is fuel for God's fire. These are the conditions for seasons of refreshing—personal revival. Do you want to see the fire?

Paul commands us to present our bodies as living sacrifices, holy and acceptable unto God (Romans 12:1). The problem with a living sacrifice is it removes itself from the altar. Therefore, we must be willing to die to self—daily literally moment-by-moment if need be. The sacrifice we present is a life willing to be used by God unconditionally. God is looking for such a sacrifice, one He can consume, cleanse, and change.

As part of presenting the sacrifice, a prayer would be made for God to accept this offering for His honor and glory. If the conditions were followed properly, the burnt offering became a soothing aroma unto the LORD. In other words, God would be pleased with the sacrifice. When our altars have been repaired, we have sought forgiveness and restoration by the blood of Christ, and we present ourselves as a living sacrifice, ready to be used and consumed however God may desire, we then become a soothing aroma unto God. These become the conditions for seasons of refreshing. The fire of God, the Holy Spirit, then begins to consume us with His presence and power, cleansing and reproofing us and filling us with Himself, changing us to be more like Jesus Christ. This is our longing and our desire; this is the revival that we so desperately need!

We close out this chapter with an old hymn by William P. Mackey entitled, *Revive Us Again* for it speaks of the conditions for seasons of refreshing.

We praise Thee, O God! For the Son of Thy love,
For Jesus who died and is now gone above

Hallelujah! Thine the glory; Hallelujah! A-men!
Hallelujah! Thine the glory; Revive us again.

We praise Thee, O God! For Thy Spirit of light
Who has shown us our Savior and scattered our night

Hallelujah! Thine the glory; Hallelujah! A-men!
Hallelujah! Thine the glory; Revive us again.

All glory and praise to the Lamb that was slain,
Who has borne all our sins, and has cleansed every stain.

Hallelujah! Thine the glory; Hallelujah! A-men!
Hallelujah! Thine the glory; Revive us again.

Revive us again; fill each heart with Thy love;
May each soul be rekindled with fire from above,

Hallelujah! Thine the glory; Hallelujah! A-men!
Hallelujah! Thine the glory; Revive us again. (15)

Recall & Application

1.   **List the three effects of forest fires.**

     _____

     _____

2.   **What was Israel's sin that brought about God's judgment?**

     _____

     _____

3.   **What are the altars that need to be repaired in your life?**

     _____

     _____

4.   **List the "requirements" in offering up the sacrifice.**

     _____

     _____

5.   **In what ways do theses "requirements" speak to you?**

     _____

     _____

6.   **When God speaks, do I listen? God spoke to me in the following ways:**

     _____

     _____

"The LORD is my shepherd; I shall not want. He maketh me to lie down in green pastures: he leadeth me beside the still waters. He restoreth my soul: he leadeth me in the paths of righteousness for his name's sake. Yea, though I walk through the valley of the shadow of death, I will fear no evil: for thou art with me; thy rod and thy staff they comfort me."

"Thou preparest a table before me in the presence of mine enemies: thou anointest my head with oil; my cup runneth over. Surely goodness and mercy shall follow me all the days of my life: and I will dwell in the house of the LORD for ever." (Psalm 23:1-6)

Chapter 4

The Provisions for Seasons of Refreshing
What Has Been Provided For Us?

Have you ever taken care of sheep? If you have, you know how much work is involved. They say sheep are among the most vulnerable of domestic animals raised in the United States. Domestic sheep are dependent on humans for protection and are very timid. Simple things like a sheet of paper blown by the wind will frighten them and a thunderstorm can set them into a panic. Sheep, even when crossing a stream, can drown without a struggle if frightened. Fire in a building can destroy the whole herd because they are to frighten to flee. (1) Sheep also, must be shifted from pasture to pasture in order to prevent over-grazing since they have a tendency to gnaw the grass to the very ground until even the roots are damaged. Sheep can be very stubborn and have a tendency to wander off from the herd and end up in hostile environment, leaving the owner to search diligently for them. (2)

Sheep demand a lot of attention and care; the shepherd, therefore, must be committed to the flock or they will perish. The shepherd must protect, lead, care for them, comfort them, and provide all their needs if he is to have a healthy, growing flock.

We are like sheep, easily disturbed, anxious, prone to wander, and sometimes very stubborn and rebellious. We often wonder into pastures of our own choosing, thinking we know what is best for our lives. We over indulge ourselves on the lush green fields of this world only to become lost and anxious, looking for someone to lead us out of our predicament. We do have a Shepherd who watches over us, who cares about our every need, who longs to fellowship with us and refresh our spirit. He is the Good Shepherd, the good shepherd that laid down His life for His sheep (John 10:11).

This chapter explores the provision for seasons of refreshing. God has provided everything we need in order to have an intimate relationship with Him. Psalm 23 speaks of the Good Shepherd's provision, preparation, and promise to us, His sheep.

The Provisions for Seasons of Refreshing.

"The LORD is my shepherd; I shall not want." (Psalm 23:1)

The LORD is my shepherd! What a statement to make! Just as the shepherd takes care of his sheep, we too have a Shepherd who takes care of us. We can rest in His care knowing He is looking out for and over us. Jesus said, *"I am the good shepherd; and I know My own, and My own know Me."* (3) He knows me, and like a shepherd, He knows my needs and cares far better than I do and will graciously provide them. *"My Own know Me."* There is an intimacy we have in knowing our Savior

80

and the willingness to trust and have faith in Him, no matter what we—as His sheep—may face. Our Shepherd watches over us day and night, as scriptures tell us, *"He that keeps thee shall neither slumber nor sleep."* (4) He is a faithful shepherd—not like a hired servant, as Jesus recorded in John 10:12-13. *"He who is a hireling, and not a shepherd, who is not the owner of the sheep, beholds the wolf coming, and leaves the sheep, and flees, and the wolf snatches them, and scatters them. He flees because he is a hireling, and is not concerned about the sheep."* Our Shepherd will protect, lead, care for, comfort, and provide for His sheep because He is the Good Shepherd who loved us enough to lay down His life for us. Let's look at how the Good Shepherd provides for us.

I. He Protects His Sheep:

Just as a shepherd would ward off intruders who seek to devour the flock, so too our Good Shepherd protects us. We have an enemy in Satan who, like a roaring lion, seeks to devour and scatter the sheep. (5) He is referred to in John 10:10 as the thief that only comes to steal, kill, and destroy. He tries to steal our joy in Christ by bringing trials and sufferings into our life. He brings in times of anguish in order to discourage and depress us, causing us to look at our circumstances rather than our Deliverer. He tries to rob us of fellowship with the Savior by enticing us to sin and rebel just as he did. He knows if we continue in sin, our hearts will become cold and distant from the Shepherd of our soul.

He comes to kill, if allowed by God, he would do that to every believer in a moment. Instead, he kills faith by using other people, circumstances, and events in order to get our focus off Jesus and unto the flesh.

By killing faith he can limit our work for God, our walk with God, and our will for God.

By killing faith he can limit our work for God, our walk with God, and our will for God. Satan comes also to destroy our testimony and our ministry. If he can get the believer to compromise in the area of morality, to fall into an adulterous affair, and live an immoral lifestyle, then he has succeeded in destroying both their ministry and witness. He seeks to destroy relationships within our family by the sin of pride, bickering, and gossip. Whether our immediate family or church family, he is ever working to tear apart the bonds that hold communities together. But Jesus said He came to give life in abundance. (6) Therefore, the Good Shepherd in protecting His sheep, has given us the power to resist the devil so he will flee from us. (7) In His divine protection, He has given us His Word to provide wisdom and strength for the battle. It is God's Word that causes the enemy to flee because His Word is true. Nothing can happen to us that God hasn't first allowed and given us the ability to overcome. Remember, we are more than conquerors through Him who loved us (Romans 8:37). God provides power in His Word and peace in the center of His will. To be without both is to be unprotected in a dangerous world. What has God provided for us for seasons of refreshing? His divine protection! The shepherd of our soul has provided that protection in the blood of the Lamb of God, Jesus.

II. He Leads His Sheep:

Jesus said He calls His own sheep by name and leads them out (John 10:3). He knows your name! What a comforting thought that out of the six billion plus people in this world, God knows your name. In a world where you are only referred to by a number, it is reassuring that we have a very personal God who calls us by name and knows us intimately. He calls His sheep with words of affection and guidance in order to direct us to the center of His will. He leads because He goes before us to prepare a way, so we may go in and out and find green pasture (John 10:9). Just as sheep listen only to their shepherd's voice, so we too must listen only to our Shepherd's voice if we are to follow His perfect way.

III.   He Cares for His Sheep:

Jesus, as the Good Shepherd, not only protects and leads His sheep, but also cares for them deeply. Just as the shepherd is concerned about everything effecting his sheep, so too, Jesus is concerned over the needs and cares which affect us. He is concerned about every detail of our lives no matter how big or small they may seem. The Apostle Peter commanded us to, *"Cast all your cares upon Him for He cares for you."* (8) We are to do this as if throwing a net over the side of a boat. In other words, throw your cares upon Him, let go of your worries and anxieties because He loves and cares for you. A little boy once asked his father in fear and uncertainty, *"Does God see everything that I do?"* The father being wise and wanting to calm the boy's fears replied, *"God loves you so much He cannot take His eyes off of you!"* This is a true statement for all of His sheep! He loves and cares for us so much He cannot take His eyes off us. Because of that care for His sheep, when one wanders off, He seeks to retrieve the erring one. And like a shepherd, He will pursue until He has restored the lost one. Jesus gave this illustration of His care, *"If any man has a hundred sheep, and one of them has gone astray, does he not leave the ninety-nine on the mountains and go and search for the one that is straying?* *"And if it turns out that he finds it, truly I say to you, he rejoices over it more than over the ninety-nine which have not gone astray."* (9) If we are to experience personal revival, we must come to an understanding of God's love and care for us.

IV. He Comforts His Sheep:

The long nights can sometimes be frightening for sheep with dangers lurking all around and being exposed to the elements.

The shepherd's presence would bring comfort to his sheep and sometimes he would sooth them by a song or playing an instrument, as David had done. Jesus, as our Good Shepherd, provides comfort to us in those same long nights with His presence. Times when we are alone and frightened, and times when we are hurting and struggling, He is there to comfort us. His Words of comfort are like a song to our heart and like a precious melody as they sooth a troubled soul. The Apostle Paul would later state, *"Blessed be the God and Father of our LORD Jesus Christ, the Father of mercies and God of all comfort; who comforts us in all our affliction so that we may be able to comfort those who are in any affliction with the comfort with which we ourselves are comforted by God."* (10) God comforts us so we might comfort others. Oh, how we need to learn from our Good Shepherd when it comes to comfort! Just as He is there during those long nights to care and comfort us, so we too need to be there for others. God's comfort in times of sorrow is truly His provision for seasons of refreshing.

V. He Provides for His Sheep:

David said, *"The LORD is my shepherd, I shall not want"* (Psalm 23:1). I shall not be in want of His protection, guidance and care, comfort or provision, for He has promised to meet my every need. (11) But there is more, for not only has He promised to meet my every need, but to satisfy me with good things. (12) In other words, He pours out His blessings on us until our spiritual cups are full and overflowing. Because He is my Shepherd and all I need is satisfied in Him, I can be content. Paul would later explain, *"I have learned to be content in whatever circumstances I am."* (13) Why? Because God is my Shepherd and He will provide and sustain me. *"I shall not want,"* literally, I shall not lack any good thing for all I desire is in Him. God has given us all we need or desire in His protection and provision, guidance and care, and His comfort and love. In Christ Jesus, God has forgiven my past, promised to meet my needs for the present, and secured my future with Him. Why then, should I be anxious or worried?

The provision for times of refreshing God has filled by supplying all of our needs and we lack nothing. But there is yet more, God sometimes prepare us for those times of refreshing from His presence by making us lie down, in other words, times when God puts us flat on our backs. He does this to restore our soul and to return us to a personal revival with Him.

The Preparations of the Sheep:

"He makes me lie down in green pastures; He leads me beside quiet waters. He restores my soul; He guides me in the paths of righteousness For His name's sake." (v. 2-3)

I. He Makes Me to Lie Down.

We have learned earlier that the shepherd, after a certain amount of time in the pasture, would move his flock. He would do this to prevent over-grazing and over-consumption. This would protect not only his sheep, but the land as well. We too are like sheep, in life's green pastures, we have a tendency to over consume, to grow fat with this world's offerings. God sometimes "make us lie down" in order to provide what we really need, revival.

We all long for the green pastures of life. Those green pastures can consist of job security, financial stability, and health—especially if facing major sickness or surgery. The green pastures can be the feeling of safety while living in an unsecured environment. They can also be a stable family relationship, where the center is love and devotion to each other. Green pastures can be a growing successful ministry, which God is blessing and lives are being changed. We have all experienced the green pastures of life, whether it is the fruit of our labors or the blessing and provision from God.

> *We desire the provision of those green pastures, but God desires our intimate fellowship with Him. We see the lush beautiful foliage in those green pastures; He sees a heart that is in need of revival. We see security and contentment, He sees coldness and indifference. We see success and wealth, He sees poverty and want. Therefore, God causes us to lie down.*

Sometimes, during the green pastures of life, we are forced to lie down. This is implied in David's statement, *"He makes me to lie down,"* because it conveys a forced rest. God sometimes allows the heaviness of trials to knock us down so we can learn to depend on Him and experience seasons of refreshing within our lives. We desire the provision of those green pastures, but God desires our intimate fellowship with Him. We see the lush beautiful foliage in those green pastures; He sees a heart in need of revival. We see security and contentment, He sees coldness and indifference. We see success and wealth, He sees poverty and want. Therefore, God causes us to lie down. When those difficult times come our way, we long for those green pastures, to return to a sedated life, a life of contentment and peace. However, God wants us to learn from those times of testing, to experience Him anew and to have a more intimate relationship with Him. I have been with friends who have gone through major illnesses or surgeries, struggling to regain their health and have heard them ask, "Why?" Through their pain and anguish, they have found the answers are not always available. But God is faithful, and in their suffering, God is teaching and training them to trust Him more. Instead of asking God why, the response should be, *"God, help me not to miss the lessons You are trying to teach me."*

These trials often come to deepen us in Him so we might draw upon His strength and find His grace sufficient for our every need. Many times, He allows trials in our lives in order to provide for us times of personal revival.

For example, Barkley was a manager of a replacement service for a major company. His job provided the green pastures of life: a steady income and a nice house with nice amenities. He was a growing Christian with a loving wife and three precious children. Suddenly and unexpectedly, the world caved in on him as he lost his job without a severance package. The green pastures now became a distant memory. He had many job interviews, yet they all came back with the same response. "We appreciate your interest in our company and you have the talent, but..." Rejection can be the worst feeling a person faces as it is the loss of his self-esteem. Men will identify with their job position for it is what they take personal pride in, and when it is taken away, depression usually sets in along with feelings of failure. Barkley faced rejection after rejection, yet he remained faithful during those times of "forced rest." He kept his eyes focused on the LORD Jesus Christ and not his circumstances. He continually prayed for God to open or close doors as He saw fit and remained steadfast in his faith. God was faithful to meet every need they had as bills were paid, often without them knowing how or by whom. The weeks dragged on and so did the interviews, each with the same response, NO! But God was faithful, and after 14 weeks of job searching, God provided a new career for Barkley. He not only found a job, but also learned to trust God during times of forced rest.

Another example, Bob owned a plumbing supply business, which was extremely successful. He too experienced the "green pastures" in life, until his company was forced into bankruptcy. Bob, being a Christian businessman, wanted to file chapter eleven in order to re-organize his debt and pay back the bank gradually. That wasn't what the bank wanted! Between the lawyers, the courts, and the debts, the finances began to dwindle. The fear of losing their home and most of everything they owed was becoming a reality. Bob and his wife were being forced to "lie down in green pastures." It was during those trials that God did a tremendous work in both their hearts. Each day God would show His faithfulness and love for them through a scripture passage or notes of encouragement from friends. God provided a Christian businessman to give wisdom and direction and the right legal counsel to advise and assist in a settlement that would be both advantageous to all parties and honored God in the process. The reorganization was allowed, the bank was paid back and Bob and his wife kept their home. Through the dark times, the times of "forced rest," what kept them going and gave them hope were the prayers of their friends and the presence of the Holy Spirit. Though going through the trial of their business failure was the hardest struggle they had ever faced, they both testified the lessons learned from God in the process were worth it all!

If you are in a "forced rest," a "lying down," may I encourage you that God still provides the green pastures and He will lead you back to them soon. This "forced rest" you are facing is God's quiet call to come back to Him. Sometimes the only way He can get our attention is when we are flat on our backs with no place to look but up! *"He makes me to lie down,"* is all part of His preparation for personal revival.

II. He Leads Me besides Still Waters.

The shepherd, after making his sheep to rest, would provide the green pastures for grazing. Then he would lead them to the quiet pools of water to quench their thirst and be refreshed. Sheep will often graze in the early morning hours to consume the dew on the grasses, since this is another source of water for them. The dew is clean, pure, and in abundance as it hangs heavy on the leaves.

So too, our Shepherd leads us to those "quiet waters," or times of meditation, reflection, and evaluation. The quiet waters are not stagnant or polluted, nor are they raging like a flood, rather they are quiet for the purpose of refreshing. In the early morning hours, His word is like the dew on the grasses, it is pure, refreshing, and satisfies the thirsty soul. It is said of the great preacher, John Wesley, that he would rise every morning at 4 a.m. and spend two hours reading scriptures and praying. In the Christian life, it is of more than passing significance to observe that those who are often the most serene, most confident and able to cope with life's complexities are those who rise early each day to feed on God's word.

Quietness and reflection can be summed up in Psalm 46:10, *"Be still, and know that I am God: I will be exalted among the heathen, I will be exalted in the earth."* To be still is to come away from the noise of this world in order to be quiet and alone before Him, listening for the Holy Spirit's still small voice. It is only when we are silent before Him that we hear His voice, as He will not compete with the noises of this world.

God leads us by the still waters in order to create a willing and obedient heart. This prepares us for seasons of refreshing, as we get our eyes back on Him and our ears open to His instruction. He leads us to those still waters that we might partake of His living water and be thoroughly refreshed.

III.   He Restores My Soul.

He makes us to lie down and leads us by the quiet waters in order to restore our soul. But there is more, many times, we, like sheep, insist on going our own way. We can be just as stubborn as sheep when we refuse to follow our Shepherd and end up in all kinds of bad predicaments. In the parable of the Prodigal Son, (Luke 15) the younger son wasted all his inheritance on riotous living. When the money was gone, so were his friends. Alone, hungry, and desperate he returned to his father asking only to be treated as one of the servants. Instead, his father welcomed him back and prepared a celebration because he was considered dead and is now alive, was lost but now is found. (14) Our gentle Shepherd came to retrieve and restore us to Himself just as the father did to his prodigal son. There are times when our hearts become cold and distant due to sin. But our Savior calls us back to Him and if we confess our sin—He is faithful and just to forgive our sin and cleanse us from all unrighteousness. (15) God's love is always calling back the wanderer and like the prodigal son, He will forgive and restore. "He restores my soul" implies a quickening; a bringing back to life what has been dormant. The Holy Spirit revives a soul that is left empty by the things of this world and gives new direction and purpose, a new thirst for Him.

He makes me, He leads me, and He restores me, this He does in order to bring revival to our soul and intimacy with our LORD. David spoke of God's instruction in Psalm 32:8, which states, *"I will instruct thee and teach thee in the way which thou shalt go: I will guide thee with mine eye."* God will teach and lead us if we are willing to follow. It is interesting to note the next verse, Psalm 32:9. God pleads with us not to be like the mule that has no understanding! In other words, don't be stubborn; rather be willing to be led and obedient to follow. God has promised to give us wisdom in every circumstance we may be in. James tells us, *"if any of you lacks wisdom, let him ask of God, who gives to all men generously and without reproach, and it will be given to him."* (16) God wants to lead us in paths of righteousness, producing our greatest joy. But there is more to Psalm 23, our Shepherd gives us the promise of His presence, comfort, security, anointing, and His reward.

The Promise of the Shepherd:

"Yea, though I walk through the valley of the shadow of death, I will fear no evil: for thou art with me; thy rod and thy staff they comfort me. Thou preparest a table before me in the presence of mine enemies: thou anointest my head with oil; my cup runneth over. Surely goodness and mercy shall follow me all the days of my life: and I will dwell in the house of the LORD for ever." (vs. 4-6)

I. His Presence.

"Though I walk through the valley of the shadow of death,"

I have nothing to fear! The promise of His presence is with us wherever we go. What a hope this is! The shepherd would watch over his sheep during the darkest of nights or the blackest of storms. Our Shepherd too, watches over us! God is with us through those lonely valleys and we will arrive on the other side victorious.

The valley of the shadow of death can mean the dark night of the soul when you are alone and anxious over difficult circumstances. It can mean the troubling and tormenting times of uncertainty—not knowing what to do or what is going to happen next. It could be the long nights of struggling in prayer over troubling issues and facing difficult days ahead. The dark night of the soul can be when a loved one is in surgery and the outcome is still uncertain. It is in these times that His presence is near and He reminds us we are not alone. He sees our tears and hears our cries. David would speak from experience when he said, *"The LORD is near to all who call upon Him."* (17) David had spent many long nights on the run from his adversary King Saul, and he knew of God's comfort in those dark times. God's presence through the long dark night gives us courage and hope, for remember, He has not given us a spirit of fear, but of power, love, and a sound mind. (18) Before we can have the mountain top experience, we must first walk through the valley. It is in those valleys that the promise of God's presence reassures and gives us the courage to go on.

The valley of the shadow of death can also mean facing death itself. Even in this the believer has the assurance of God's presence. We have nothing to fear of shadows, for shadows are but a vapor expelled by the light of His glorious presence. The confidence of every believer is knowing our walk is *through the valley*—not lost in it. Literally, it is a gentle walk from this world to join His. When facing death we know Jesus will be with us to change our mortal bodies into a body like His. Paul would say with the shout of triumph, *"But when this perishable will have put on the imperishable, and this mortal will have put on immortality, then will come about the saying that is written, "DEATH IS SWALLOWED UP in victory. "O DEATH, WHERE IS YOUR VICTORY? O DEATH, WHERE IS YOUR STING?"* (19)

We all will walk through valleys sometime in our life. Whether they are valleys of trials, sufferings, or the valley of death itself, we will go through it. And either way, we have the assurance of His presence with us and therefore, we do not fear. The promise of His presence in dark valleys is part of the provision for seasons of refreshing He provides for us.

II. His Comfort.

Thy rod and thy staff they comfort me.

The rod, in some instances, was a short thick branch used as a club for defense. In other instances, it was a long thick branch used for support and protection. The shepherd would use this to ward off would-be predators trying to attack the herd and sometimes he would use it as a disciplinary tool for his sheep. The staff was a long branch with a hook at the end and used for many purposes. The shepherd would lean on his staff when tired for support, he would use it to draw his sheep near to

> *Though many have tried to destroy God's Word, stop God's Word, and even change God's Word, it still remains today the source of all power and hope.*

inspect them, and he would use it to lift a lamb out of a predicament. The rod and the staff brought comfort to the sheep because they represented the power and presence of the shepherd.

God's Word is His rod to us today; His Word is powerful and sharper than any two edged sword. (20) It will bring conviction to the lost and hope to the child of God. His Word changes lives and gives direction and purpose to all who will study it diligently. God's Word is powerful; it casts out devils, gives courage to the fainthearted, and strengthens the faithful. Though many have tried to destroy God's Word, stop God's Word, and even change God's Word, it still remains today the source of all power and hope. Jesus said, heaven and earth would pass away but His Word shall never pass away—that alone speaks of the everlasting power of the Word of our God. (21)

The staff would represent the shepherd's presence and would symbolize the shepherd's comfort. Our staff is found in the presence of the Holy Spirit in our lives. He is our comforter. When we are tired and worn out by this world, He is there to encourage and strengthen us. Because He is our comforter, we can lean on Him and trust Him for wisdom and guidance. The shepherd would use his staff to guide his sheep along the pathways, so too our Comforter uses His staff (the Word of God) to lead and guide us.

"Thy rod and thy staff," the presence and the power of God are with us wherever we go, this is His promise and provision to us. No wonder David could say in the valley of the shadow of death, *"Thy rod and Thy staff they comfort me."*

III.   His Security.

"Thou prepares a table before me in the presence of my enemies."

97

God has provided for us all things pertaining to life and godliness. (24) He has provided all things required for body and soul and for time and eternity—such a benefactor is our great Shepherd! The "table prepared" speaks of God's great provision ahead of time, for He knows our every need and has anticipated the results. Note that the table is prepared in the presence of enemies! When a soldier is in the presence of his enemies, if he eats at all, it is usually in haste and he is always ready to fight if necessary. But here, the table is properly displayed and the food diligently prepared, nothing is hurried, or in confusion and panic. Even though the enemy is at the door, God is preparing a table for us. The Christian sits down in perfect peace and communes with his Savior. The Child of God will have enemies, as our LORD has warned us, but He has promised us perfect peace within. Though those who wish us harm may surround us, we are perfectly secure in His presence. The prophet Isaiah would echo these thoughts, *Thou wilt keep him in perfect peace, whose mind is stayed on thee: because he trusteth in thee. Trust ye in the LORD forever: for in the LORD JEHOVAH is everlasting strength."* (23) The promise of being secured in Him, even though the world may be in turmoil, is another part of His provision for times of refreshing.

IV.   His Anointing.

   "Thou anointest my head with oil; my cup runneth over."

The shepherd would pour an oil mixture over his sheep to protect them from infestations and to soothe the wounds caused by the biting insects. This would bring great comfort to the sheep during the summertime months when parasites were at their worst.

In this phrase, David recalled the time of his anointing by Samuel as the future king of Israel. Scripture records when Samuel took the horn of oil and anointed David in the midst of his brothers, the Spirit of the LORD came mightily upon David from that day forward (1 Samuel 16:13). David's cup was overflowing, meaning God had poured out His Spirit upon David without reserve.

In the same way, God pours His Spirit out on us! Paul would urge us to be, filled with the Holy Spirit continually. (24) Every Christian is a priest, but he cannot execute the priestly office without unction, and therefore we must go day by day to God the Holy Spirit, in order that we may have our heads anointed with oil afresh and anew. The promise we have is the anointing of the Holy Spirit, the soothing, comforting, and filling which He graciously provides.

> *He showers us with His loving-kindness and divine favor. What a marvelous thought to realize, that each and everyday we have His grace and mercy given to us in abundance.*

V. His Blessing and Reward.

"Surely goodness and mercy shall follow me all the days of my life: and I will dwell in the house of the LORD forever."

God's promise to us is His grace and mercy to be showered upon us all the days of our lives. His grace, means His unmerited favor, which is precisely what we do not deserve, yet it is given freely in Christ Jesus. His mercy, meaning not giving us what we deserve—His wrath and condemnation, is turned away. Instead, He showers us with His loving-kindness and divine favor. What a marvelous thought to realize each and everyday we have His grace and mercy given to us in abundance. We also have the promise of spending eternity with our LORD Jesus Christ, never to be separated, only to dwell in His presence forever. AMEN!

Application:

The provision for seasons of refreshing, is God providing everything we need in order to experience a personal revival with Him. In His provisions He will protect, lead, comfort, and care for us. Because He is our Shepherd, we have all we need. In providing for us seasons of refreshing, He sometimes brings a forced rest upon us, only to restore us in due time for His name's sake. Lastly, we looked at the promise of His presence in those dark, lonely valleys. He has given us the *rod and staff* representing the comfort of His power and presence, which is with us always. And the promise of His security, by preparing a place of communion—the table, with us even though we are surrounded by enemies. We also have the promise of His anointing, the Holy Spirit, symbolized by the oil. Lastly, we have the promise of His reward that we may dwell with Him forever. All of this He has provided for us. What should our response be but to desire for and seek after times of refreshing from the presence of the LORD.

An old hymn written by William B. Bradbury that ends this section so elegantly is *Savior, Like a Shepherd Lead Us*, and mediate on the words as you read them.

Savior, like a shepherd lead us,
Much we need Thy tender care;
In Thy pleasant pastures feed us,
For our use Thy folds prepare:
Blessed Jesus, Blessed Jesus,
Thou hast bought us, Thine we are;
Blessed Jesus, Blessed Jesus,
Thou hast bought us, Thine we are;

We are Thine; do Thou befriend us,
Be the Guardian of our way;
Keep Thy flock from sin defend us,
Seek us when we go astray;
Blessed Jesus, Blessed Jesus,
Hear, O hear us when we pray;
Blessed Jesus, Blessed Jesus,
Hear, O hear us when we pray;

Thou hast promised to receive us,
Poor and sinful though we be;
Thou hast mercy to relieve us,
Grace to cleanse, and pow'r to free;

Blessed Jesus, Blessed Jesus,
early let us turn to Thee;
Blessed Jesus, Blessed Jesus,
early let us turn to Thee;

Early let us seek Thy favour;
Early let us do Thy will;
Blessed LORD and only Savior,
With Thy love our bossoms fill;
Blessed Jesus, Blessed Jesus,
Thou hast loved us, love us still;
Blessed Jesus, Blessed Jesus,
Thou hast loved us, love us still (25)

Recall & Application

1.   List the "provisions" by the Good Shepherd.

_____

_____

2.   List the "preparations" by the Good Shepherd.

_____

_____

3.   List the "promises" made by the Good Shepherd.

_____

_____

_____

4.   How has God's presence and power affected your walk with Him?

_____

_____

5.   How has God provided for seasons of refreshing in your life?

_____

_____

6.   When God speaks, do I listen? God spoke to me in the following ways:

_____

_____

Applying Part One

The Desperation for Seasons of Refreshing:
What have we learned?

Personal revival begins when we see our desperation for God. The tyranny of the urgent has left us with a desperate heart longing for seasons of refreshing in our lives. We have paid the price of neglecting our families, friends, and our relationship with God in order to gain success, status, and the luxuries of this world. The end result is a life frustrated and empty that is longing for meaning and purpose. The search has led us to more "things" as we seek to fill the void with materialism. It has also led many into inappropriate relationships leading to adulterous affairs, as they look for someone to lift them out of the bonds of despair. Satan always has an "understanding somebody" waiting near by to provide the "answers" to the emptiness and confusion of life. It is a vicious cycle, we are empty inside and so we try to fill it with something or someone; it only produces more emptiness and even more frustration. Yet, the answer can only be found in the person of Jesus Christ. When we see the need for seasons of refreshing in our lives, He then moves on our hearts, drawing us back to Him.

> *Revival is the hearts cry for God to invade our lives again with His presence and to fill us with His Spirit.*

Personal revival is our hearts' cry for God to invade our lives again with His presence and to fill us with His Spirit. It is a heart's longing to know Jesus and to have an intimate relationship with Him constantly and continually. It is to thirst for God, like a deer panting for water and will not be satisfied until her thirst is quenched. We will not be satisfied until our "soul" thirst is quenched by His love and grace. When we long for Jesus Christ to again fill our lives, we are coming to an understanding of seasons of refreshing.

Personal revival is desiring the fire of God to consume us, cleanse us, and to change us forever! Like a raging forest fire sweeping across acres of timber, we long for God's fire to sweep over our churches, our communities, and our nation. We know there are conditions to God's revival fire. Altars that are broken down, need to be repaired. We must become like kindling for the Master's use, ready to be consumed by His fire at any time. We present ourselves as the living sacrifice, offered up for His praise and glory. These are the conditions for seasons of refreshing and when they are met—God will send His holy fire to consume the sacrifice.

Personal revival is realizing God has provided everything we need to walk in fellowship with Him. We lack nothing because

He protects, cares, leads, and comforts us like a good shepherd would his sheep. His promises give hope to the discouraged, comfort to the sorrowful, and strength to the helpless.

This is what we have learned. The desperate, which long for seasons of refreshing, will apply these truths.

Part Two: The Direction to Seasons of Refreshing

Direction = **1.** An instruction or series of instructions for doing or finding something. **2.** An "order" or "command." **3.** The line or course along which a person or thing moves.

"I will instruct thee and teach thee in the way which thou shalt go: I will guide thee with mine eye." (Psalm 32:8 KJV)

"Thou shalt guide me with thy counsel, and afterward receive me to glory." (Psalm 73:24 KJV)

"And the LORD will continually guide you, And satisfy your desire in scorched places, And give strength to your bones; And you will be like a watered garden, And like a spring of water whose waters do not fail." (Isaiah 58:11)

"Come to Me, all who are weary and heavy-laden, and I will give you rest. "Take My yoke upon you, and learn from Me, for I am gentle and humble in heart; and you shall find rest for your souls. "For My yoke is easy, and My load is light." (Matthew 11:28-30)

Chapter 5

Experiencing Seasons of Refreshing
Rest for Your Soul:

Tired?

Are you tired—worn out mentally, emotionally, and spiritually? Are you discouraged from giving, ministering, serving, and leading? In your ministry, do you feel alone and empty from pouring yourself out in order to build others up? You are not alone in your struggle; for many servants of Christ are facing these same issues. I often wonder how Jesus felt after ministering to so many and yet facing rejection day after day. In the Gospel of Mathew, Chapter 11, Jesus was ministering in the towns of Chorazin, Bethsaida, and Capernaum. These towns should have welcomed Jesus warmly, since His fame had spread from nearby communities. They saw Him perform many miracles and heard His message about the kingdom of heaven. Yet they would not believe, as scripture records, *"He came unto His own, and His own received Him not."* (1) With a heavy heart, He rebuked them for their unbelief and proclaimed a very sobering message, *"I say to you that it shall be more tolerable for the land of Sodom in the Day of Judgment, than for you. For if the miracles had occurred in Sodom which occurred in you, it would have remained to this day."* (2) Then, in the midst of His pronouncement of judgment upon their unbelief, He turned to the remnant that believed and spoke words of encouragement. He was reminding them they are not alone in their service to God.

Many times, we feel we are alone. We continue to pour ourselves out in ministry to people who just don't seem to hear or care. Elijah, the prophet, felt he was the only one left serving God in all of Israel, his response was, *"I have been very zealous for the LORD, the God of hosts; for the sons of Israel have forsaken Thy covenant, torn down Thine altars and killed Thy prophets with the sword. And I alone am left; and they seek my life, to take it away."* (3) Elijah was lonely, frustrated, and "burned out" from facing the overwhelming circumstances of life. We have all felt that way, overwhelmed with tasks, frustrated from the lack of help from others, and tired of ministering to people who won't believe or who simply don't respond. You may be a youth pastor, a Sunday School teacher, an elder, or a deacon, burdened with the responsibility and left alone to accomplish the task. You have poured yourself out, given until you cannot go on, ministered until there was

> *When we become afraid, we have a tendency to forget the past miracles God has done for us. We forget how often God has delivered us from disaster, protected us from evil, and brought victory over those who met us harm.*

nothing left to "minister", and now feel "burned out." If you are there right now, take courage, Jesus has an invitation for you to experience seasons of refreshing from His presence. Let's examine those feelings of being "burned out" and see how God directed Elijah to experience times of refreshing, personal revival, in his life again.

...And I Alone Am Left.

In Chapter 3, as part of the conditions for seasons of refreshing, Elijah, the prophet, had won a tremendous victory over the prophets of Baal. They had prepared a sacrifice and labored all day, calling on their god to answer by consuming the sacrifice with fire, and the end results were *"there was no voice, no one answered, and no paid attention"* (1 Kings 18:29). Elijah then repaired the altar of the LORD, which had been broken down, arranged the wood, and prepared the sacrifice. Then he prayed, and God answered by fire. So amazed were the people they began to cry out, *"The LORD, He is God, the LORD, He is God."* (4) Revival had come to the people present that day and Elijah was a part of it. What a tremendous victory! However, it is usually after a tremendous victory God has brought, when Satan begins to enter in to discourage God's chosen servants. Elijah was no different and neither are we. Queen Jezebel made a vow, before the day was over, Elijah would be put to death. When we become afraid, we have a tendency to forget the past miracles God has done for us. We forget how often God has delivered us from disaster, protected us from evil, and brought victory over those who met us harm. Elijah was quick to forget the fire that fell consuming the sacrifice. He didn't recall how God provided during three and half years of famine and drought. It slipped his mind the miracles God did through him, such as restoring the life of the widow's son. (5) Instead, he fled in terror as scripture records, *"And he was afraid and arose and ran for his life."* (6) Tired and defeated, he laid down under a juniper tree wishing to die. A great victory was now a distant memory and joy was replaced with depression and self-pity. What happened? Elijah, like all of us so often do, took his eyes off God and focused them upon people and circumstances. Had the God, who just answered by fire, vacated His throne? Did the Sovereign One of the whole universe suddenly become powerless? Did the queen's vow catch God by surprise like Elijah? Did God's hand become to short to save? In all these instances, the answer is an overwhelming NO! Yet, that becomes our thinking and we become defeated and spiritually burned out as a result.

Alone, under the juniper tree, wishing to die and feeling sorry for himself, Elijah falls asleep. The Bible records that the angel of the LORD came and to awaken him to food and water in order to prepare him for a journey to Horeb, the mountain of God. (7) There, on the mountain, he would have an encounter with the Holy One of Israel. Mount Horeb was regarded as a holy place where God dwelt. It is here, after forty days of journey, Elijah had been led to experience times of refreshing from the presence of God.

In 1 Kings 19, God confronted Elijah with a very serious question. *"What are you doing here, Elijah?"* (8) Elijah's response is one of frustration and depression; *"I have been very zealous for the LORD, the God of hosts; for the sons of Israel have forsaken Thy covenant, torn down Thine altars and killed Thy prophets with the sword. And I alone am left; and they seek my life, to take it away."* (9) You can hear the pain and frustration of his struggling. He is saying literally, *"God, I am fighting this battle all alone and I can not go on."* Many of us can relate to those feelings that Elijah was going through.

God wanted to get Elijah's eyes off himself and unto the ministry that he had been called. The same with us, God wants an outward focus on Him and not an inward focus on our circumstances. God told Elijah to get out of the cave of self-pity and stand by the cleft, for God was going to reveal His glory to him. First, there was a strong, violent wind shattering the rocks. But God was not revealed in the wind! Next, there was an earthquake, a violent shaking of the whole mountain. Yet, God was not in the earthquake! Then, there was a ball of fire that rushed by, possibly cinching Elijah by the scourging heat. Yet, God was not revealed in the fire! Finally, there was the still, small voice as a gentle breeze whispering to Elijah. Once again, God was there to get Elijah's eyes focused back on Him. God often speaks to us in a still small voice. It is a voice of hope and encouragement giving direction and purpose. It is not violent, harsh, or abusive. In that still small voice, God confirmed Elijah and gave him a new commission, to anoint three people who would be agents of God's judgment on a nation that had rejected Him and His prophet. First, Elijah was to go and anoint a new King of Aram, who would later be used to bring chastisement upon Israel. Secondly, he was to anoint a new King of Israel. At that moment, God had sealed the fate of King Ahab and Queen Jezebel. They had been weighted in the balances and were found wanting, for their lives soon would be over. God had just pronounced Elijah the victor over those who had sought his life and brought idolatry into the land. Thirdly, God told Elijah to anoint Elisha as his heir replacement. In other words, a student to teach and tutor in the school of the prophets, one who would encourage and support Elijah. In these two statements, God had given Elijah victory, hope, and encouragement to continue on in his ministry. There was more, for God didn't want Elijah to think he was alone in his struggle against the forces of evil. God reminded Elijah, there were 7,000 in Israel who had not bowed down to Baal or worshipped him. (10)

Notice how God provided those seasons of refreshing for Elijah. First, He gave him what he needed most—rest, refreshment and a warm meal. Then he drew Elijah back to a quiet place, Mt. Horeb, in order to reveal Himself and give Elijah a new ministry. God desires to do this for all His servants who are tired and burned out from the pressures of life. He wants us, as Elijah did, to experience times of refreshing from the presence of the LORD. Let's apply these principles to our text in Matthew 11:28-30 as we long for the rest God provides.

I. The Invitation:

"Come to Me, all who are weary and heavy-laden," (Matthew 11: 28-30)

Jesus offers an open invitation for all who are worn out from this world's struggles, to come unto Him. We may try to find someone or something else to revitalize us, but there is only one who can give rest to our souls, and He is our Savior. He is our source of strength and he gives grace to help in time of need. The invitation is to "come," and not "to do", as He wants us to yield in submission and let Him work in and through us. We are invited to come freely, not under obligation or coercion, but "to earnestly desire Him" to take our cares.

The invitation is for all those who are weary and heavy-laden. Being weary means to labor to the point of fatigue. It is being physically tired from our toils of life, and in need of rest. The workday continues to get longer as companies downsize, placing more work on those who are left. It is pushing oneself to the extreme and the result is complete physical exhaustion. The pressures of job, family, and ministry continue to increase and the weight of these often becomes overwhelming. We, at times, are at a loss on how to deal with these issues. Jesus, however, gives us an invitation to come unto Him with these burdens and cares and lay them down before Him. It is a personal invitation for each of us to come and surrender all.

Weariness also comes from internal exhaustion. It is carrying burdens that wear us down emotionally and spiritually. Burdens, which we were never meant to carry by ourselves, yet they are on our hearts continually. Burdens, such as, family members who are in sin and rebellion, a friend or loved one going through a divorce, the uncertainty of a job situation, the struggles of finances, etc. All of these and more weigh heavily upon us, feeling like a huge rock upon our shoulders.

In our preceding story, Elijah became weary and heavy-laden as he too, started to carry burdens he wasn't meant to carry. When he responded, *"and I alone am left,"* Elijah thought the battle was his alone to fight. All of Israel had forsaken God and he was left to defend God's righteousness. In his eyes, all the pressure of winning back an erring nation was on him. No wonder he became discouraged! We will too, when we think we are alone in our service for God or the outcome of our ministry is based upon our own labors.

Sometimes we become like packing mules loaded with heavy supplies. One slip and all the supplies would come tumbling off. One slip, and we come apart at the seams on everyone around us. Again, this is why Jesus gives us the invitation, *"Come unto Me."*

Being weary also speaks of fatigue from trying to please God. It is carrying the yoke of self-righteousness, or the keeping of rituals and laws, codes or customs. This is done in an effort to try to please God by our "good works." It is the never-ending burden of self-sacrifice and self-discipline in order to be more acceptable to God. Jesus came to provide us His righteousness solely by grace, apart from any law. Thereby, lifting the yoke of bondage completely from us. Part of experiencing seasons of refreshing begins with understanding we are complete in Christ and lack nothing. The Apostle Paul said, *"For in Him dwells all the fulness of the Godhead bodily. And you are complete in him."* (11) The invitation is to come and enjoy His rest and comfort and be sustained by His presence. This is a gift given freely by the Holy Spirit, based on what Jesus has done on the cross for us.

For some, being weary and heavy laden is the result of carrying the load of their personal sin. The guilt and anguish you may bear and the baggage you may carry, can all be forgiven by responding to the Saviors invitation. His plea is *"Come unto Me,"* as He will abundantly pardon and cleanse you from all your iniquities.

When do we experience the seasons of refreshing in our lives? When we are willing to come unto Jesus and give Him those burdens we are carrying and to surrender those heavy loads. The invitation is clear, *"Come unto Me all who are weary and heavy laden,"* as He is the only One who can truly give us rest.

II. The Implementation:

"And I will give you rest."

What kind of rest does Jesus give? To answer this, let's look at several definitions for the word; "rest."

To *rest,* means a cessation from labor, motion, action or exertion. In other words, it is a period of time when we stop all we are doing in order to find rest and be rejuvenated. We can find rest in Christ when we cease from our activities and study His Word. We are rejuvenated when we take time to be with God and commune with Him. He commands us to, *"Be still, and know that I am God: I will be exalted among the nations, I will be exalted in the earth."* (12) God wants us to be silent before Him and rest in His presence in order to experience times of refreshing. He is asking us to take the time to learn and grow in knowledge of Him.

To *rest,* means freedom from anxiety and worry. Jesus gives us rest from these by promising never to leave nor forsake us. He is always there to encourage and strengthen us and He is there to handle our burdens and cares. Paul told us, *"Be anxious for nothing, but in everything by prayer and supplication with thanksgiving let your requests be made known to God. And the peace of God, which surpasses all comprehension, shall guard your hearts and your minds in*

Christ Jesus." (13) What a promise for us to claim and what a rest He provides!

To *rest*, is finding comfort in that which is fixed and settled. We can find true rest in Christ's finished work on the cross. He settled the sin issue once-and-for-all. We don't have to live a life full of strict laws, codes, and customs in order to please God. We don't have to live in uncertainty about our salvation and our relationship with God. If you are uncertain about your relationship with God, receiving Christ as your Savior and asking Him to forgive your sins can settle it. We can be confident of our salvation in Christ because it is based on the Word of God. Our eternal destiny is forever settled and we can rest in that assurance.

To *rest*, is being confident and trustful. We can face the challenges of tomorrow knowing God is with us. We have the confidence God is working in us daily to make us more like Christ. We trust in His plans for our life since they are for good and not evil. He will not lead us astray as Paul would state, *"He who began a good work in you will perform it until the day of Christ Jesus."* (14) God is working in and through us in order for us to grow in faith and be confident in Him.

> To rest, is learning, reposing, and depending.

To *rest*, is learning, reposing, and depending. We are learning to rely on the faithfulness of God since He has promised to meet our every need. He is teaching us to trust

Him and to not let worry or anxiety be a part of our lives. When we rely on His promises, learn from His teachings, relax in His care, and depend on His guidance, He will provide the rest we are longing for.

This gives us an idea of the rest Jesus provides. It is a rest to revive our hearts and it is promised to all who will come. Are you are among those who are wearied of their sin and heavy laden with guilt? Are you are tired physically, emotionally, and spiritually from the load you are carrying? Are you are in need of His perfect rest and the joy of His presence again? Then, His rest is what you seek and it will bring peace to a troubled soul and hope to the discouraged. The command is clear, *"Come unto Me and I will give you rest."* This is the hope we have in Christ. His rest is waiting to be implemented if you are ready to apply it to your life.

III.   The Inspiration:

"Take My yoke upon you, and learn from Me, for I am gentle and humble in heart; and you shall find rest for your souls. "For My yoke is easy, and My load is light."

"Take My Yoke," like the command to "come," is an invitation from the Savior. He is asking us to be joined to Him like two oxen were by their yoke. The "yoke" was part of the harness used to pull a cart or a plow and was the means by which the animal's master kept it under control and guided it in useful work. A student is under the yoke of his teacher, in order

that he might receive instruction and be guided along. Children are under the yoke of their parents, as they are trained in the way they should go. Taking Christ's yoke is to be joined to Him and to place yourself under His Lordship and care. When we take Christ's yoke, He then frees us of ours. The yoke of bondage, whether to sin and self or to the cares and demands of this world, He loosens and removes. His yoke is easy and the burden or weight of it is light. He is not an overwhelming or cruel taskmaster; He doesn't put demands on us we cannot bear. His yoke is one of authority over our lives. When we "take His yoke," we experience His refreshing.

"Learn of Me," is another command for us. We are to learn of and from Him, by faithfully studying and applying His Word. For example, the young Jewish student would set faithfully and obediently under his Rabbis' teaching, in order to become his disciple. We are also commanded to faithfully and obediently sit under our Master's teaching, that we may become His disciples. We are to learn also by doing; James tells us to be doers of the Word and not just hearers only. (15) We learn by studying His Word, we learn by faithfully doing what He has commanded us, and we learn by observation, seeing Jesus' compassion for the sick, the poor, the lost, and the destitute. We can see how He responded when falsely accused or slandered, and how He gave His life as a ransom for many. All of this and more we are to learn of Him and from Him to do the

same thing. This is what Jesus met when He said, *"learn of Me."*

To learn of Jesus, takes time and patience; yet, that is what He asks us to do. Paul told his young disciple, Timothy to, *"Study to show thyself approved unto God, a workman that needeth not to be ashamed, rightly dividing the word of truth."* (16) We are to set apart time to study and meditate on scriptures in order to be approved by God. We are to know scriptures in order to be discerning and not fall into error. We are to be diligent students, earnestly seeking after and applying truth to our lives. A friend once told me, this Book, (the Bible) will either keep you from sin or sin will keep you from this Book. Time and patience are a part of maturing and growing in love for the Savior. It takes time to learn of Him by listening to His teachings. When Jesus said, *"learn of Me,"* I believe He meant to faithfully study, learn, and grow in His Word. We cannot learn from our Master if we only meet with Him once a week or less. Can you imagine trying to pass a college course if you only studied once a week? You might get lucky and pass through it, but this course is on life. In order to succeed, you must apply what you've learned, and to learn you must study diligently.

God gave Joshua the keys to success when He said, *"This book of the law shall not depart from your mouth, but you shall meditate on it day and night, so that you may be careful to do according to all that is written in it; for then you will make your way prosperous, and then you will have success."*

(17) Note that the conditions are to read, meditate, and do. The results are, your ways will prosper and you will have success. Who wouldn't want these keys in their lives? Like Joshua, we have this scripture and many more promises God's Word provides for us to prosper and have "good success." It comes down to this, if we love the Savior, we will faithfully devote ourselves to studying His Word. We cannot experience, and He will not send, true revival apart from using His Word. Therefore, when we are willing to take "His yoke and learn from Him" then we can experience seasons of refreshing in our lives.

"I am gentle and humble in heart." In Christ, there is meekness and humility and all is smooth, even, peaceable, and quiet. Isaiah said, *"And the work of righteousness shall be peace; and the effect of righteousness quietness and assurance forever."* (18) As we grow in the knowledge of Christ, we realize He is the gentle shepherd that watches over us. Being gentle means being considerate or kind, not harsh, severe, demanding, or overtaxing. He is humble in heart, meaning He is patient, not given quickly to anger. He endures our resistance and rebellious attitude to Him, still calling us to take His yoke and learn. When we finally realize His yoke is easy and His load is light, then submission to Jesus Christ brings the greatest liberation a person can experience. Adam Clark's Commentary on this passage in Matthew concludes with this thought; *"My Gospel imposes nothing that is difficult; on the contrary, it provides for the complete removal of all that which oppresses*

and renders man miserable, viz. sin. The commandments of Christ are not grievous. Hear the whole: Thou shalt love the LORD thy God with all thy heart, and thy neighbor as thyself. Can any thing be more congenial to the nature of man than love?—such a love as is inspired by God, and in which the soul rests supremely satisfied and infinitely happy? Taste, and know, by experience, how good the LORD is, and how worthy his yoke is to be taken, borne, and loved. This most tender invitation of the compassionate Jesus is sufficient to inspire the most diligent soul with confidence." (19)

"Take My yoke and learn of Me," is our inspiration to follow His command. When we are faithful to submit and willing to learn, He will give rest to our souls. *"For My yoke is easy and My load is light,"* to submit to His Lordship is truly a light load for us to carry.

> *When do we experience seasons of refreshing? When we are willing to come unto Him with our burdens and our cares, which weigh so heavy upon us, and surrender them.*

Application:

When do we experience seasons of refreshing? When we are willing to come unto God with our burdens and our cares and surrender them. We started this chapter by talking about being spiritually tired and burned out by bearing burdens we were not meant to carry. We looked at Elijah the prophet, and how he thought he was alone in serving God. When confronted by his enemy, Jezebel, he became afraid and fled into the wilderness. Yet, God intervened with rest and encouragement.

Discouragement and depression always seem to be near when we face difficult times. When we get our eyes off of the LORD and onto our circumstances, we become frustrated with life. But what are the answers to those times of frustrations, discouragement, and depression? Where do we find the hope, courage and strength to go on? How can we find rest for our soul when we are carrying baggage within? The answer can only be found in the invitation by Jesus Christ to *"Come unto Me."* When we respond to His invitation, He gives rest from those burdens and peace within our soul.

In our story of Elijah, when he fell asleep under the juniper tree, "the angel of the LORD" came and ministered to him. The "angel of the LORD," in the Old Testament, was often referred to as the pre-incarnate Christ. Here, we have the LORD Jesus Christ providing food, water, and rest in order to prepare Elijah for his journey. God is always meeting our needs, be it food and water for the physical needs, or rest for our soul. He is always there to provide. The invitation by Jesus is still there for all to come. *"Come unto Me, all who are weary and heavy-laden, and I will give you rest."* This is an open invitation, for He has made His rest readily available and accessible. When do we experience seasons of refreshing? When we respond to His invitation and come. We give Him our burdens and cares and He gives us His yoke of hope and rest. What an exchange!

When we take His yoke and willingly submit to His Lordship, then we begin to learn from Him. We can face the trials of life knowing we will not miss the lessons God wants to teach us. The command to *"learn of Me,"* is to "diligently apply" God's Word to our lives. When we do this, we will truly find rest for our souls. Experiencing seasons of refreshing from the presence of the LORD begins when we apply His invitation and come unto Him.

Fanny Crosby wrote a hymn, entitled *Jesus Is Calling;* that summarizes Christ's invitation for all to come unto Him and find rest for their souls. Mediate on these lyrics as you read them.

> *Jesus is tenderly calling thee home—calling today,*
> *calling today; Why from the sunshine of love wilt thou*
> *roam Farther and farther away?*
>
> *Calling today, Calling today, Jesus is calling*
> *is tenderly calling today.*
>
> *Jesus is calling the weary to rest—calling today,*
> *calling today; Bring Him thy burden and thou shalt be*
> *blest: He will not turn thee away.*
>
> *Calling today, Calling today, Jesus is calling*
> *is tenderly calling today.*
>
> *Jesus is waiting; O come to Him now—Waiting today,*
> *waiting today; come with thy sins; at His feet lowly*
> *bow; Come, and no longer delay.*

*Calling today, Calling today, Jesus is calling
is tenderly calling today.*

*Jesus is pleading; O list to His voice: Hear Him today,
hear Him today; They who believe on His name
shall rejoice; Quickly arise and away,*

*Calling today, Calling today, Jesus is calling
is tenderly calling today.* (20)

Recall & Application

1.   **What is the invitation that Jesus gives?**

_____

_____

2.   **Describe the rest that Jesus provides?**

_____

_____

3.   **What did Jesus mean when He commanded, "learn of Me?"**

_____

_____

4.   **List the areas in which you are feeling alone in and burned out on?**

_____

_____

5.   **What must you do to experience the seasons of refreshing?**

_____

_____

6.   **When God speaks, do I listen? God spoke to me in the following ways:**

_____

_____

"In the year of King Uzziah's death, I saw the LORD *sitting on a throne, lofty and exalted, with the train of His robe filling the temple. Seraphim stood above Him, each having six wings; with two he covered his face, and with two he covered his feet, and with two he flew. And one called out to another and said, "Holy, Holy, Holy, is the* LORD *of hosts, The whole earth is full of His glory." And the foundations of the thresholds trembled at the voice of him who called out, while the temple was filling with smoke."*

"Then I said, "Woe is me, for I am ruined! Because I am a man of unclean lips, And I live among a people of unclean lips; For my eyes have seen the King, the LORD *of hosts." Then one of the seraphim flew to me, with a burning coal in his hand, which he had taken from the altar with tongs. And he touched my mouth with it and said, "Behold, this has touched your lips; and your iniquity is taken away, and your sin is forgiven."*

"Then I heard the voice of the LORD*, saying, "Whom shall I send, and who will go for Us?" Then I said, "Here am I. Send me!" And He said, "Go, and tell this people: 'Keep on listening, but do not perceive; Keep on looking, but do not understand.' "Render the hearts of this people insensitive, Their ears dull, And their eyes dim, Lest they see with their eyes, Hear with their ears, Understand with their hearts, And return and be healed."*

*"Then I said, "*LORD*, how long?" And He answered, "Until cities are devastated and without inhabitant, Houses are without people, And the land is utterly desolate," "The* LORD *has removed men far away, And the forsaken places are many in the midst of the land. "Yet there will be a tenth portion in it, And it will again be subject to burning, Like a terebinth or an oak Whose stump remains when it is felled. The holy seed is its stump."*
(Isaiah 6:1-11)

Chapter 6

The Purpose of Seasons of Refreshing
Seeing God for Who He is.

"It was the Best of Times and it was the Worst of Times:"

Like the beginning of Charles Dickens's *Tale of Two Cities* the events surrounding the believers in America can be summed up by the very best of times and the very worst of times. It is the best of times because we've experienced a sustained period of economic prosperity that has lasted longer than any other time in our history. We have enjoyed, literally seasons of prosperity, unlike any generation before us. Many Americans have vast amounts of income at their disposal. In many areas the unemployment levels have dropped below 5% creating a demand for workers, even delaying openings of businesses and service industries. The younger generation of today has no concept of the word "recession," as they have had unlimited opportunities for income (providing they are willing to work). They have also had vast amounts of income given to them by their parents with little or no restraints. It is a time of excess, and it is called the "best of times."

It is also the worst of times as we live in a society that has lost her soul. Today there is no distinguishing between right and wrong because our moral compass is blurred. Any type of moral restraint is considered divisive and old fashioned; hence drugs, alcoholism, pornography, and homosexuality have become a way of life. What the American public sees on television, in public, or listens to—no longer shocks them. We've become desensitized to the perversion and immorality that surrounds us. The phrase, *"rules are only made to be broken,"* has become the cry of this age. This generation can be summed up with this statement, *"there is no fear of God before their eyes"* (Romans 3:18). The holiness of God has become a mockery by many; His laws are openly ridiculed and broken with no thought of the consequences. The ACLU, and similar groups, continues to get all references pertaining to God removed from public display in order to remove any and all moral restraints from society. This generation, unlike any other generation, is in desperate need for a move of God.

These times have produced feelings of uncertainty for many. They know the "good times" cannot continue as Americans have spent their way into massive amounts of debt. The loss of their income due to company downsizing or closure would be devastating. There is a feeling of uncertainty as our culture has become anti-Christian and persecution of believers could be on the horizon. There is anxiety over wondering if God will remove His hand of blessing and protection from our country since we continue to reject His plea for repentance. We all experience these feelings of uncertainty; however, we must not let fear and anxiety control our lives.

Isaiah's Uncertainties:

Isaiah faced life's uncertainties after the death of Israel's righteous king. His nation, like ours, was going through the best of times and the worst of times. In 2 Chronicles 26, Uzziah was the King, and he reigned for 52 years bringing prosperity to the Kingdom of Judah. Uzziah was a tremendous military leader, by conquering his enemies and securing peace for the Kingdom, his fame spread throughout the land. To keep peace, he had built fortified towers in the wilderness to be prepared against any surprise attack. He had trained an elite army with the latest and best of military armament. He had designed and implemented a weapons technology that was unheard of in those days. God had blessed the reign of Uzziah, because he diligently sought the LORD his God.

Under Uzziah, Judah's economy was prospering. Trade routes were established and the land was yielding abundant harvests. Uzziah's kingdom mirrored the times of prosperity similar to the reign of King Solomon with vast amounts of wealth and beauty. It truly was the best of times. The people lived in security because no enemy was powerful enough to dare attack. They enjoyed wealth and economic good times, living life to its fullest, but the uncertainties were starting to come in.

Scripture records at the height of Uzziah's military strength, his heart became proud and he acted unfaithful to the LORD. He had entered into the holy place in the temple of the LORD to burn incense on the altar of incense, a function reserved only for the priest. The priests were to be the mediators between God and man. In his arrogance, he thought he could supersede their role. This was an act of pride and self-righteousness, as he thought he was above God's ordinances and commands. When confronted by the priest to leave immediately, he responded with anger and defiance. At that precise moment, the historian Josephus recorded, an earthquake shook the temple, causing a fissure in the wall allowing a ray of sunlight to pierce through, landing on Uzziah's face instantly turning into Leprosy. (1) He was removed from the temple and spent the rest of his life as a leper in a separate house outside the walls of Jerusalem. (2) Solomon, in all his wisdom, pronounced the verdict when he said, *"Pride goes before destruction, And an haughty spirit before stumbling"* (Proverbs 16:18). During his final days, his son Jotham, became the acting king in Uzziah's place.

Uzziah was now dead. The cracks in the armor of security were beginning to show, the people had lost their commitment to the LORD their God. They once again began to offer sacrifices in the wilderness to gods who didn't exist. And as the Psalmist stated, we become like the gods we serve. (3) They became cruel, cold, distant, selfish and indifferent to the real and true God.

Isaiah was faced with these uncertainties and in this time God called Isaiah to a ministry that would change his life forever.

Fresh Vision:

I. Seeing God for Who He is.

"In the year of King Uzziah's death, I saw the LORD sitting on a throne, lofty and exalted, with the train of His robe filling the temple. Seraphim stood above Him, each having six wings; with two he covered his face, and with two he covered his feet, and with two he flew. And one called out to another and said, "Holy, Holy, Holy, is the LORD of hosts, The whole earth is full of His glory." And the foundations of the thresholds trembled at the voice of him who called out, while the temple was filling with smoke." (Isaiah 6:1-7)

In times of uncertainty, the one certain thing is the faithfulness of the LORD our God! Isaiah saw the LORD in all His glory! Ezekiel would later confirm, within his own vision, that the LORD sitting upon the throne had the form of a man. (4) But John, in his Gospel, would be bold enough to declare that it was Jesus who Isaiah really saw. (5) The pre-incarnate Christ was revealed in all of His glory and majesty, high and lifted up for all to behold. The Apostle Paul so rightly exclaimed, *"That at the name of Jesus every knee should bow, of things in heaven, and things in earth, and things under the earth; And that every tongue should confess that Jesus Christ is LORD, to the glory of God the Father"* (Phil 2:10-11). The train of His robe filled the temple completely, allowing Isaiah to see for himself that the temple, as well as the very heavens could not contain Him. (6) The long flowing robe would speak of Jesus' royalty, majesty, and splendor, as the sovereign King.

The Seraphim hovered above the robe, each one with six wings. Two of the wings covered their face to indicate their humility before God. With two more, they covered their feet to indicate their service before God and with two they would use to fly—indicating their proclamation of God's character. The proclamation they shouted back and forth was a doxology of uninterrupted praise. *"Holy, Holy, Holy, is the LORD of hosts, The whole earth is full of His glory."* God is the Holy One who is above and beyond the world. The one true light of spotless purity that is perfect in all that He is or does. His glory is manifested in His holiness echoed for all to hear and understand. The whole earth is full of His glory! Creation shouts the glory of God!

When the Seraphim began to shout their doxology, the foundations of the temple trembled. Filled with the awesome presence and power of God, the temple quaked at the very sound of the word "holy." As the Seraphim's song reverberated, smoke began to engulf the temple. The smoke gives us a glimpse into the character of the Seraphim, as their name means "to set on fire" or "burn up." Ezekiel, in his vision, would see the Seraphim as "burning coals of fire" as bright as lightning flashes darting back and forth. (7)

Isaiah saw all this in a moment of time and was overwhelmed. Who wouldn't be? To see God in all of His glory and majesty would give us a different perspective of how holy He really is. It would change the way we approached Him in our worship and prayer. It would impact us on how we ministered and served others, and it would alter the way we conducted our lives. It changed Isaiah's life forever!

II. Seeing Ourselves for What We Are.

"Then I said, "Woe is me, for I am ruined! Because I am a man of unclean lips, And I live among a people of unclean lips; For my eyes have seen the King, the LORD of hosts." (Isaiah 6:5)

Isaiah exclaimed the pain of seeing himself in the light of God's holiness. In an instant of time, God exposed all the hidden sins of

> *Before the prophet could pronounce "woe" upon a nation in rebellion, the "woe" must first come to the prophet!*

Isaiah. All the secret passions and filthy communications, the coarse jokes, and the foolish talking, which are so often done without thinking, came to light. Suddenly he was exposed, seeing himself as he really was, as we really are, and the cry is "WOE IS ME!" Isaiah saw himself in the light of God's holiness as shameful; even his righteousness was nothing more than filthy rags. (8) Jesus would describe those conditions with the example of the Laodicean church, because they were poor, wretched, miserable, blind and naked. (9) That description is for all of us since we are completely helpless, hopeless, and lost apart from Christ.

The vision of God's holiness, majesty, and splendor made Isaiah see himself as a sinner in need of divine cleansing. Before the prophet could pronounce "woe" upon a nation in rebellion, the "woe" must first come to the prophet! He had become the subject of God's pronouncement because of sin. The unclean lips would symbolize the attitude, actions, and lifestyle of an individual in rebellion against God. Jesus said, *"For the mouth speaks out of that which fills the heart"* (Matthew 12:34). Isaiah also identified himself as one having unclean lips, literally, a mouth that would both speaks blessings and harsh, cruel, and vindictive cursing. This also, his people did without remorse.

We, like Isaiah, need a fresh vision of who God is in order to see ourselves for what we really are. Leonard Ravenhill, the famed Revivalist, once said, *"If we were half as spiritual as we think we are, we would be going to the house of the LORD in sackcloth and ashes. We would fill the altars on Sunday morning with weeping and repentance for a lifestyle that is in direct opposition to God."* (10) Yet, we will not because of our pride, and that is why revival tarries! Isaiah saw God in all of His holiness and saw himself in all of his debasement.

He did not make excuses for his lifestyle, or justify his position. Rather he did the only thing he could do, he cried out to God! Until we begin to see the exceedingly "sinfulness" of sin in ourselves, we will not know or experience true seasons of refreshing from the presence of the LORD. God will not send true revival within our nation until He first begins it within His church. Peter echoed that statement when he said, *"Judgment must first begin in the house of God."* (11) Our prayer should be for God to give us a fresh vision

> *Fire consumes, cleanses, and changes often times permanently. The fire of God consumed Isaiah with love, forgiveness, and a changed life forever!*

of who He is, in order that we may see ourselves for what we are, and begin to seek cleansing and forgiveness.

When Isaiah cried out in confession of his sin, one of the Seraphim took a coal from the altar of incense and touched his lips, purging and purifying him of his sin. The Seraphim assured him, *"This has touched your lips; and your iniquity is taken away, and your sin is forgiven."* The fiery coal symbolizes the "burning" or "purging" of sin held by Seraphim, which means to "consume or burn up." In the illustration of a forest fire, (chapter three) fire consumes, cleanses, and changes, often times permanently. The fire of God consumed Isaiah with love, forgiveness, and a changed life forever!

Isaiah would long remember this vision, for throughout his prophecies, he would refer to God as the "Holy One of Israel." (12) Seeing God's holiness brought about a death to self for Isaiah, as he stood in the midst of the presence of the Holy One, listening to the praises by pure lips.

We too, need to cry out for our Savior to burn away the chaff and consume us in the Father's love. Isaiah's vision of God changed his life forever, as he saw God for who He is and then saw himself for what he was. This alone should be enough to direct us to seasons of refreshing, but there is more. After the vision God gave Isaiah a new ministry.

Fresh Calling:

"Then I heard the voice of the LORD, saying, "Whom shall I send, and who will go for Us?" Then I said, "Here am I. Send me!" And He said, "Go, and tell this people: 'Keep on listening, but do not perceive; Keep on looking, but do not understand.' "Render the hearts of this people insensitive, Their ears dull, And their eyes dim, Lest they see with their eyes, Hear with their ears, Understand with their hearts, And return and be healed." Then I said, "LORD, how long?" And He answered, "Until cities are devastated and without inhabitant, Houses are without people, And the land is utterly desolate," "The LORD has removed men far away, And the forsaken places are many in the midst of the land. "Yet there will be a tenth portion in it, And it will again be subject to burning, Like a terebinth or an oak Whose stump remains when it is felled. The holy seed is its stump." (Isaiah 6:8-11)

Isaiah's feelings of uncertainty were shattered after he encountered the One who holds the future. The LORD Jesus Christ had revealed Himself in all of His glory and majesty to Isaiah, changing him forever. When God put the call out for a prophet, Isaiah was quick to respond. Experiencing God's mercy and forgiveness should motivate us for service as well. It did for Isaiah, without thought of consequences.

Isaiah heard the voice of the LORD in a commanding call, *"Whom shall I send, and who will go for Us?"* Isaiah without hesitation, quickly responded, *"Here am I. Send me!"* Note what he didn't say! Phrases like: *"I have to pray about it first."* *"I don't think I'm being led into this ministry." "I'm not sure I have the time." "I'm too busy!" "Can't you find someone else?"* NO! His response was, *"send me, LORD, you have forgiven and cleansed me of all my sin how can I not serve you the rest of the days of my life?"* Isaiah didn't hesitate to respond and he didn't care about the cost. His desire was to serve God with reckless abandonment. The Apostle Paul echoed those same thoughts on serving Christ, *"But whatever things were gain to me, those things I have counted as loss for the sake of Christ. More than that, I count all things to be loss in view of the surpassing value of knowing Christ Jesus my LORD, for whom I have suffered the loss of all things, and count them but rubbish in order that I may gain Christ"* (Phil 3:7-8). Isaiah's response of *"here am I, send me,"* was as a school child waving his hand, hoping not to be over looked. He was willing and eager to be used by God.

The call Isaiah received was difficult at best. A prophet's life was a hard life; he would preach messages no one wanted to hear. He would not have people coming up to him after the service and telling how they appreciated his message. Nor would he be invited as a guest speaker to special meetings.

Instead of compliments and accolades, he would get threats and accusations. Wanted for today: Prophets from God!

Prophets were always alone, for he would spend much time in solitude with God. In the desert places he would be tried in the furnace of affliction until he emerged with a heart broken for the things that broke God's heart. His cry would be for repentance or judgment would certainly come, and his burden would be to do the will of God regardless of the outcome. He had to be willing to die daily in order to bring forth the fruit God desired.

God's commission to this young prophet was, *"Go, and tell this people: 'Keep on listening, but do not perceive; Keep on looking, but do not understand. Render the hearts of this people insensitive, Their ears dull, And their eyes dim, Lest they see with their eyes, Hear with their ears, Understand with their hearts, And return and be healed."* His calling was to go back to the people and warn them. He was purged by the Seraphim for his unclean lips, but "this people" would not be purged! Their hearts would be rendered insensitive, hardened, made fat, without feeling for the operations of divine grace. To this wrath, Isaiah would deliver up his people for their continuance in sin, and consequently the LORD would proceed to shut the door of repentance. Nevertheless, He directed the prophet to preach repentance because this did not preclude the possibility of salvation to individuals.

Isaiah asked, *"How long, LORD?" "How long will they listen but not hear? How long will they see but not understand? How long will they continue in a lifestyle contrary to God's law? How long will they walk in disobedience and rebellion?"* That question Isaiah asked, we might ask as well. How long will a nation continue to murder the unborn and not receive Divine judgment? How long will a nation mock God's holiness and not receive His wrath? How long will people flaunt a lifestyle that God called an abomination and not experience His chastening hand? Leonard Ravenhill compared modern day America to ancient Sodom and came up with this description.

- Sodom had no churches = we have thousands.
- Sodom had no Bible = we have millions.
- Sodom had no preachers = we have ten thousand plus ten thousands.
- Sodom had no Bible schools = we have hundreds.
- Sodom had no prayer meeting = we have thousands.
- Sodom had no gospel broadcasts = as a nation we are richly blessed with Christian broadcasts.
- Sodom had no history of God's judgment to warn it of danger = we have volumes of them.
- Sodom perished in spite of all these disadvantages.
  = America today is living only by the mercy of God. (13)

The answer Isaiah received was, *"Until cities are devastated and without inhabitant, Houses are without people, And the land is utterly desolate, "The* LORD *has removed men far away, And the forsaken places are many in the midst of the land."* This passage contains an outline of the history of Israel to the end of time. Israel, as a nation, was indestructible by virtue of the promise of God. But the masses of people were doomed to destruction through the judicial sentence of God, and only a remnant would be converted to inherit their glorious future. This law of blessing, sunk in the depths of the curse actually inflicted, still prevails in the history of the Jews. The way of salvation is open to all as individuals find it, but the great masses are hopelessly lost.

Until the cities are left desolate; Isaiah must have carried this thought with him all the days of his life. Knowing a few, a remnant, would listen and respond to the message of repentance, but the majority would go on with their lives without regard, thought, or fear of the consequences. Much like today, the warnings are clear, the message has gone out, but only a few have responded. And the rest...To those who, like Isaiah, are called to preach an unpopular message, remember, *"Moreover it is required of stewards, that one be found trustworthy"* (1 Corinth 4:2). God simply asks of His prophets to be faithful, the outcome is and always has been, His responsibility.

Application:

What happens when we see God for who He is? Isaiah encountered God in all of His majesty and holiness and saw himself in all of his unrighteousness. Crying out in repentance, Isaiah was cleansed by the fire of God's love. When we see God for who He is, our response will also be repentance and contrition.

> *God is looking for people who He can break, mold, and use for His glory and purpose.*

How does one have an encounter with God? We may not have the vision Isaiah had or see the glory of God as Moses did, but we can know and experience Him through the Holy Spirit. God has given to each believer the ministry of the Holy Spirit; literally, God is living in us! Jesus said the Holy Spirit would abide in the believer, forever. (14) Paul tells us we are the Temple of the Holy Spirit and God is dwelling within us! (15) To gain a fresh vision of who God is then begins with time in prayer. When we earnestly seek Him, and are willing to be exposed by His holy light of conviction, when we are willing to repent and return to Him, then we will understand the purpose of seasons of refreshing from the presence of the LORD.

The purpose of seasons of refreshing is God wanting to give us a fresh vision of who He is. In giving this vision, He instills in us His desire and purpose for us. God is looking for people who He can break, mold, and use for His glory and purpose. God used Isaiah mightily and all of eternity will show forth the results of his faithfulness to the call. He was just a man like us, who desired to be used by God, whom God broke in order to give him a heart for the things God has a heart for. As we desire the seasons of refreshing in our lives, let's remember that God grants those seasons in order to bring about His purpose and plan in and through us. God wants to give us times of refreshing through His presence, but they are conditional upon our repentance and returning to Him. God through Jeremiah the prophet stated, *"And you will seek Me and find Me, when you search for Me with all your heart. And I will be found by you."* (16) If we are willing to seek Him earnestly in prayer, the fresh vision and the fresh calling are available.

We close this chapter with a song of praise entitled, *Majestic Sweetness Sits Enthroned* by Samuel Stennett—it speaks to what we have just studied.

Majestic sweetness sits enthroned
Upon the Savior's brow;
His head with radiant glories crowned,
His lips with grace o'er flow
His lips with grace o'er flow

No mortal can with Him compare,
Among the sons of men;
Fairer is He than all the fair
Who fill the heav'nly train,
Who fill the heav'nly train.

He saw me plunged in deep distress,
And flew to my relief;
For me He bore the shameful cross,
And carried all my grief,
And carried all my grief.

To Him I owe my life and breath,
And all the joys I have;
He makes me triumph over death,
And saves me from the grave,
And saves me from the grave. (17)

Recall & Application

1. **What sin brought Leprosy upon Uzziah?**

_____

_____

2. **What does it mean to "see God for who He is?"**

_____

_____

3. **Describe what it means to "see ourselves for what we really are?"**

_____

_____

4. **What did God call Isaiah to do and what was the outcome?**

_____

_____

5. **According to 1 Corinthians 4:2, God asks of you to be what?**

_____

_____

6. **When God speaks, do I listen? God spoke to me in the following ways:**

_____

_____

And they were continually devoting themselves to the apostles' teaching and to fellowship, to the breaking of bread and to prayer. And everyone kept feeling a sense of awe; and many wonders and signs were taking place through the apostles.

And all those who had believed were together, and had all things in common; and they began selling their property and possessions, and were sharing them with all, as anyone might have need.

And day by day continuing with one mind in the temple, and breaking bread from house to house, they were taking their meals together with gladness and sincerity of heart, praising God, and having favor with all the people. And the LORD was adding to their number day by day those who were being saved.
(Acts 2:42-47)

Chapter 7

The Results of Season of Refreshing:
What Happens when God Fills a Heart?

The Coming of Pentecost:

It was a day like no other. It had been fifty days since the resurrection of the Messiah and Jerusalem was filled with people in anticipation of celebrating the Feast of weeks, Pentecost. The Torah had called for every male to be in Jerusalem on that day. Not only was it a time of rejoicing since the barley harvest was in—it was a celebration that on this day, the Law was given to the Jews. God had miraculously delivered them out of Egypt and led them to Mount Sinai where He gave them the most holy of instructions, the Torah.

But this Pentecost was different from previous celebrations, as Jesus had told His disciples to tarry in Jerusalem until they were filled with power from on high. (1) The Disciples were not sure what that meant, but never-the-less they did as He had requested. In His departing to heaven, Jesus told them, *"You shall receive power when the Holy Spirit has come upon you; and you shall be My witnesses both in Jerusalem, and in all Judea and Samaria, and even to the remotest part of the earth"* (Acts 1:8). A bold commission, to tell the world the message of salvation through Jesus, the Messiah! But they would do it in the strength and power of the Holy Spirit.

Jesus told them many things concerning the Holy Spirit. For instance, He would be called their Comforter, literally, one called along side to help. He would be their source of strength, courage, and hope. The Holy Spirit would also be their teacher and would tutor them on scriptures, and He would bring to remembrance all things that Jesus had done. The Holy Spirit would abide with them forever! This was comforting to them but hard to understand. In the past, the Holy Spirit was selective and fell upon certain individuals that God had seen fit to use. But not every believer in Yahweh (God) was filled. Now, the promise was for all who called upon the name of the LORD, would be saved and indwelt with the Holy Spirit.

This was enough to have the Disciples waiting in anticipation for the coming of the Holy Spirit. But did they truly understand what all this meant? Did they realize the power that would engulf them? Were they prepared for the changes in their lives the Holy Spirit would bring? Did they understand the promise Jesus made to them? *"Greater works than these shall you do because I go to the Father."* (2) They probably didn't have a clue, and neither do we.

The Arrival of Pentecost:

The place was called the Upper Room. It was a meeting place for the Disciples, and others, who gathered there to pray and wait upon the arrival of the Holy Spirit. But how would He come and what would be the results? These questions were constantly on their mind, as they prayed and waited.

Suddenly there came from heaven—a noise, like a rushing, mighty wind that filled the whole house. The wind was invisible, mysterious, powerful, and yet, refreshing as it typified the Holy Spirit. These circumstances were similar, yet different from the past, as God had used the forces of nature to announce this extraordinary event. When the Torah was given there was lightning and thunder. When the Messiah was born, there was a star in the heavens. And when Christ was crucified, there was a great earthquake. Now, there was the sound of the wind, as if a violent storm was approaching. Only this wind was the power and the presence of the *Ruach HaKodesh*, the Holy Spirit sent from God.

Scripture records that there appeared, to those who had gathered, "tongues of fire" distributing themselves, and resting upon each one of them. (3) The Jewish believers would draw the parallel to the first Pentecost, where signs and wonders accompanied the giving of the Torah at Mount Sinai. (4) During the giving of the Law, there was smoke, fire, and a thick cloud that concealed the mountain. The mountain literally shook, as the blast of the Shofar sounded louder and louder, and then the voice of God was audibly heard by the entire nation. The Midrash, (5) speaks of flames of fire, which came to each individual at Sinai. Jewish tradition tells that the children of

Israel not only heard the LORD's voice, but also saw the sound waves as they emerged from the LORD's mouth, visualizing them as a fiery substance. Each commandment spoken by the LORD, would travel around the whole camp, speaking to each one in their native language so that all the nations present that day would hear and understand the Torah of God. (6)

On this Pentecost, the tongues of fire distributed themselves among the believers and they began to speak in languages they had no prior knowledge of. The Jewish people, gathered from all over the world to celebrate the festival, suddenly began hearing the message of Yeshua, Jesus as the Messiah, in their own native tongue. Jews and Gentile converts from all over the known world, were hearing what great deeds God had done through Jesus, their Messiah, for the first time. Many wondered, *"What does this mean?"* Still others were saying, *"The languages are the voices of the drunken."* But the tongues of fire continued as it consumed, cleansed, and changed the faithful forever.

Peter stood to speak to the multitude, but his voice was different now then before. There was a new power within his spirit, a new sense of boldness as he proclaimed the risen LORD. This same Peter, who had denied the LORD just days ago, was now preaching with great resolve. So much so, that every eye was upon him and every ear was attentive to his message, as he quoted from the Holy Scriptures. Then, as if he had his sword in his hand again, he zeroed in on their hearts with this final statement, *"Therefore let all the house of Israel know for certain that God has made Him both LORD and Christ—this Jesus whom you crucified"* (Acts 2:36). Their hearts were pierced through by the convicting power of the Holy Spirit and many cried out, *"Brethren, what shall we do"* (Acts 2:37)? And Peter said to them, *"Repent, and let each of you be baptized in the name of Jesus Christ for the forgiveness of your sins; and you shall receive the gift of the Holy Spirit"* (Acts 2:38). That day three thousand souls were added to the Kingdom.

The Return to Pentecost:

The day of Pentecost, the birth of the church, had begun with the commission to take the message of the death, burial, and resurrection of Jesus Christ to the ends of the earth. This message would go with the power, signs, and wonders of the Holy Spirit. The early church was alive, filled with excited people who were amazed at the marvelous work God was doing among His faithful.

But what about today? Can we have another Pentecost? Can we have a great moving of God within our churches, to fill us afresh and anew with the Holy Spirit? I believe the answer is YES! However, are we willing to meet the conditions for the seasons of refreshing that we long to have? Are we willing to wait upon God, literally, to tarry until we are filled with power from on high? Leonard Ravenhill gives this observation on why we need to tarry:

- "For humiliation and for time for a confession of our too-long-a-time satisfaction with our own works.

- To get our spiritual eyes refocused on the holiness of God and the lostness of men.

- To linger until we have a broken and contrite spirit.

- To prove we can master the claims of this materialistic age in which we live.

- To hear again the living voice of the living God.

- To show our utter disregard for our own efforts and our complete dependence upon the living God for deliverance in this sin-dominated age.

- To convince our skeptical friends that we love the will of God, that we long for the favor of God, and that we seek the power of God with more zeal than we can put into our business lives and with greater hunger than we have for food.

- For a sorrowful confession of sin and pleading of cleansing thorough the blood of Christ. In the divine presence, vows would be made to put wrongs right and to remain submissive to God's revealed will. I believe that then the Spirit would fall." (7)

If we are to experience another Pentecost within our churches, we must realize God doesn't always fit into the box we've tried to put Him in. To often we have made a list of what the Holy Spirit can and cannot do within our fellowships. We proclaim certain gifts are no longer in use for this day. Yet in doing so, we have limited God on what He can and will do in and through us. When God visits His people with another Pentecost, He will pour out all of the gifts of the Holy Spirit to be used as He sees fit and not on what meets the current theology. With these gifts, He will use people to do the impossible because He is a God that makes all things possible.

To experience another Pentecost within our churches, today, we must be willing to get

> *For too long we have been content with our spiritual pride and self- sufficiency that we really don't know or don't care to know, what a moving of the Holy Spirit is.*

out of our comfort zone and expect God to move in our midst! For too long we have been content with our spiritual pride and self-sufficiency that we really don't know or don't care to know, what a moving of the Holy Spirit is. We have limited the Holy Spirit's working within our lives and we have grieved Him. Many times our unbelief and preconceived notions on the moving of God's Spirit has left our churches dead or dying. Wanted! A heaven sent move of God to shatter the status quo!

For too long Christians have went to their churches expecting nothing from God and getting exactly what they have desired. NOTHING! In the early church, they gathered in anticipation, expecting God to do the miraculous. In some of our churches today, there is the struggle to keep awake long enough to hear the closing prayer. In the early church, souls were being saved continually and the church was growing tremendously. Today, most of the church growth is coming from people leaving their dead, existing church and going to a vibrant, Spirit filled one. This is not bad in itself, but where is the moving of the Holy Spirit in bringing lost souls into the kingdom? Is it because there is no desire on our part to see God move in the hearts of the lost and dying?

The early church gathered in one accord to pray and encourage one another. In many of our churches today there are divisions, hardness of heart, and bitterness, that result in splits and strife. In the early church there was repentance, confession, and confrontation of sin. In many of today's churches sin is excused and even condoned. In the early church, men and women were filled with the Holy Spirit and lived holy lives. In many of today's churches people are filled with self and live self-indulgent lives.

If we are to experience another Pentecost, we must be willing to do as the early church did. They gathered together to pray and wait for the falling of the Holy Spirit. In other words, they gathered in anticipation and in expectation as they earnestly sought after God. Jonathan Edwards was a man who earnestly sought after God. In his diary he wrote, *"I feel an urgency of the soul to be...emptied and annihilated, to lie in the dust and be full of Christ alone, to love Him with a holy pure*

love, to trust in Him, to live on Him, and to be perfectly sanctified and made pure with a divine and heavenly purity."
(8) It is said of Edwards that he wept as he preached, broken for the things that breaks God's heart, the lostness of men. Many have tried to duplicate his message, *"Sinners in the Hands of an Angry God,"* but never with his results. Why? Because he was a man filled with the Holy Spirit and burdened in prayer. We cannot do what he did because we won't do what he did, and that is to earnestly seek after God.

If we are to understand what it means to experience another Pentecost, we must first look at what Pentecost did to the early believers.

The Results of Pentecost:

I. A New Spirit of Boldness:

"Then Peter, filled with the Holy Spirit..." (Acts 4:8)

When the Holy Spirit fell upon the faithful, there was a new sense of boldness in proclaiming the truths of God's Word. On Pentecost, when Peter was filled with the Holy Spirit, he preached a soul-stirring message that broke the hearts of those who listened. Peter, who constantly was speaking without thinking, now boldly proclaimed the message of salvation. *"Repent, and let each of you be baptized in the name of Jesus Christ for the forgiveness of your sins; and you shall receive the gift of the Holy Spirit"* (Acts 2:37). Just days earlier, Peter filled with fear, denied his LORD. Now, he was filled with power and a new love that only the Holy Spirit could give him. Peter and John would face the unbelieving Sanhedrin with confidence and certainty, as they confronted them with the fact, *"There is salvation in no one else; for there is no other name under heaven that has been given among men, by which we must be saved"* (Acts 4:12). The Sanhedrin had the authority to have Peter and John beaten and cast into prison with that statement, but it did not stop them. Unashamed, fearless, and bold described their actions and attitudes, as they were men filled with the Holy Spirit.

The leaders of the Sanhedrin knew Peter and John were just common fishermen. There was nothing special about them. They didn't have all the degrees behind their names like they had. But they observed them to have great confidence because they had been with Jesus. (9) The Holy Spirit had given Peter and John a new boldness that chased away all the doubts and uncertainties, giving them a confidence in Christ which could not be shaken. The Holy Spirit can do that within us as well!

What is needed today is a new sense of boldness! Proclaiming the message of salvation with power and conviction, to stand as Paul did and exclaim, *"I am not ashamed of the gospel, for it is the power of God for salvation to everyone who believes."* (10)

II. A New Source of Commitment:

"And they were continually devoting themselves to the apostles' teaching and to fellowship, to the breaking of bread and to prayer" (Acts 2:42).

The results of Pentecost were seen not only in a new spirit of boldness, but also in a new source of commitment. The believers devoted themselves to the apostles teaching. In other words, they gave themselves to the careful and diligent study of God's Word. They listened and applied truth to their lives and grew in their knowledge of Jesus. The apostles too, gave themselves to the study of scripture, so as the Holy Spirit imparted to them, they in turn imparted to the people.

The results of another Pentecost will also result in a renewed hunger for God's Word. There will be a longing to study and apply God's truth to our lives. Our cry will be as Jeremiah the Prophet was, *"Thy words were found, and I did eat them; and thy word was unto me the joy and rejoicing of mine heart"* (Jeremiah 15:16). The Holy Spirit will be our tutor as we wait upon Him.

The early church, filled with the Holy Spirit, devoted themselves to fellowship with other believers. They desired to be around people who loved Christ and no longer wanted to participate with or associate among those who were profane in actions and attitudes. They were in every sense, new creatures in Christ. They devoted themselves to fellowship, meaning they were committed to the welfare of each other.

When the Holy Spirit fills a believer today, the same is true. There is the desire for fellowship, to share a common faith with each other. The Holy Spirit will knit hearts together in one accord to strengthen the body and build up the faith. He will fill His people with love and compassion for one another. Jesus said, *"By this all men will know that you are My Disciples if you love one another"* (John 13:35). The results of another Pentecost will be a renewed desire to fellowship with other believers, and in that fellowship will be the desire to love, encourage, and meet the needs of each other.

Scriptures record after Pentecost, they devoted themselves to the breaking of bread together. The thought here is to take part in the LORD's supper or to share communion with each other. The filling of the Holy Spirit put within each of them a desire to remember the LORD's suffering and to do it with reverence. The results of another Pentecost will be to take us back to the cross and see the sufferings of our Savior afresh and anew. Realizing that the sufferings He endured, He did for love.

They also devoted themselves to prayer— earnest, heart felt,

> *They prayed expecting, they prayed out of need, they prayed with a burden, they prayed with brokenness, and they prayed with power.*

Holy Spirit—led prayer. They prayed fervently and often, and they prayed with such intensity that the room they were gathered in was shaken. (11) They prayed expecting, they prayed out of need, they prayed with a burden, they prayed with brokenness, and they prayed with power.

If we are to experience another Pentecost, there must be a desire and a burden to pray. To pray expecting, to pray out of need, to pray with and for brokenness, to pray with power, to pray fervently and to pray often. It has been said that little prayer will produce little results, much prayer will produce much results.

"They gave themselves to prayer." The early church sought the presence and the power of God in their lives. Is it any wonder the book of Acts was filled with miracles of people being healed, the lame walking, and thousands being saved? If we are to see the same results we must do as they did, give ourselves to prayer.

III.   A New Sense of Awe:

"And everyone kept feeling a sense of awe; and many wonders and signs were taking place through the apostles." (Acts 2:43)

After Pentecost, they had a sense of awe at the wonders God was doing. There was a sense of anticipation and expectation with God, as He moved within their midst. They gathered together to share the LORD's supper, they gathered together to listen and to study scripture, they gathered together to fellowship and encourage each other, and they gathered expecting great things from God.

In Acts chapter three, Peter and John, filled with the Holy Spirit, healed a lame man and all the people, *"were filled with amazement."* (12) As a result, in Acts chapter five, the people were carrying the sick out into the streets, hoping even the shadow of Peter might fall on them so they would be healed. This was the result of a moving of God within the hearts and lives of people. There was a sense of anticipation and expectation, as they brought the sick, afflicted, and those with unclean spirits to the apostles *"and they were all being healed."* (13) Scripture records a multitude of men and women were constantly added to their number that is why there was a sense of awe among the people. (14) Souls were being saved, people were being healed, the afflicted were being delivered, and lives were being changed forever. They were witnessing the fire of God fall and the results were lives being consumed by the Holy Spirit, hearts being cleansed from sin, and souls changed forever.

When times of refreshing come from the Holy Spirit to the church, there will be sense of awe at the greatness of God. Souls will be saved, as believers reach out to the lost and compel them to come in and hear the Word. People will be healed and delivered from sins that bind them. Relationships will be restored through forgiveness and restoration. Emotional hurts and scars, borne for many years, will be healed. The prodigal will return to seek an intimate relationship with Jesus Christ. And lastly, God will bring healing to many of the sick and afflicted. Physical healing will indeed take place as God moves to free His people of their afflictions.

"There was a sense of awe." This should be our anticipation every time believers come together, to fully expect God to do the impossible. Do you have a sense of awe of God?

IV.   A New Spirit of Generosity:

"And all those who had believed were together, and had all things in common; and they began selling their property and possessions, and were sharing them with all, as anyone might have need." (Acts 2:44-45)

The filling of the Holy Spirit produced within believers a new Spirit of generosity. They had all things in common as they shared what God had blessed them with. They sold their property and possessions in order to meet the needs of others. God did not require them to do this; rather they did it as a result of being filled with the Holy Spirit. The fruit of the Spirit is love—unconditional, sacrificial love. It is a willingness to give and expect nothing in return. And this they did willingly and wantonly with joy, as a testimony of a changed life.

They gave to those who had a need. Peter, the rest of the Apostles, and the faithful gave generously without holding back.

No longer was there the selfish "me" centered lifestyle, rather it was a life committed to sharing the love of Christ to all.

The results of a new Pentecost will produce the same Spirit of generosity. Many will give out of a heart of love, a soul of compassion, and a will surrendered to the Lordship of Christ. A person, filled with the Holy Spirit, will realize that all they have, own, or posses, belongs to God. The tight fisted grasping and keeping of "things" will be yielded to a generous, giving heart that seeks only the glorification of the Savior.

V. A New Strength of Fellowship:

"And day by day continuing with one mind in the temple, and breaking bread from house to house, they were taking their meals together with gladness and sincerity of heart," (Acts 2:46)

The Holy Spirit, at Pentecost, gave the believers a new strength in their fellowship and a growing love for one another. The things that strengthen them far outweighed that which divided them. Gone was the pettiness and bickering. Instead, their focus was on the love of God and sharing of what they had.

They shared the elements of communion together, they shared their meals together, and they shared what they had with each other. Jesus had told His Disciples, *"A new commandment I give to you, that you love one another, even as I have loved you, that you also love one another. "By this all men will know that you are My disciples, if you have love for one another"* (John 13:35-36). The Holy Spirit gave the believers of the early church that kind of love and as a result,

> *The filling of the Holy Spirit in today's church will produce equal results. Wrongs will be made right, forgiveness and restoration will take place, and attitudes and actions will be changed.*

their numbers were increasing daily! The lost saw their love and commitment to and for each other, and were drawn into the fold. In a matter of a short time, all of Jerusalem was filled with new believers in Christ. In doing so, the Sanhredin complained to the Disciples, *"you have filled Jerusalem with your teaching."* (15)

The filling of the Holy Spirit in today's church will produce equal results. Wrongs will be made right, forgiveness and restoration will take place, and attitudes and actions will be changed. Churches once split will be re-united as they publicly confess sin and repent. The world will truly see believers caring for and loving one another just as Jesus commanded. Our focus will be on reaching the lost with the Gospel of Jesus Christ as we cry out for souls to be saved and revival to sweep our land. Wanted! God to send us another Pentecost!

VI. A New Attitude of Worship.

`*"Praising God, and having favor with all the people. And the LORD was adding to their number day by day those who were being saved."* (Acts 2:47)

After Pentecost, there was a new spirit of boldness, a new source of commitment, a new sense of awe, a new spirit of generosity and a new strength of fellowship. There was also a new attitude of worship. When they gathered together to learn from the apostles teaching, to pray, and to share all things with each other, they also worshipped and praised God. The Holy Spirit had filled them with the desire to worship in "Spirit and truth" just as Jesus said. (16)

When one is filled with the Holy Spirit, a new attitude of praise will flow out of their being as they rejoice in the great things God has done. Worship will be the desire of their heart, as they seek to draw close and learn from Him. The Psalmist David said, *"I will bless the LORD at all times; His praise shall continually be in my mouth"* (Psalm 34:1). The inward attitude of praise will be filled with songs and worship to the LORD, and the outward action of praise will be the sharing of scriptures, encouraging one another.

The early church showed charity to all. They were, as Jesus said, the salt of the earth and the light of the world (17) and people were drawn to their lifestyle. The fruit of the Spirit, love, joy, peace, patience, kindness, goodness, faithfulness, gentleness, and self-control was evident in the believers lives, which shown forth as a light in the midst of darkness. Those lost and dying saw that light as their only hope. The love of Christ was reflected in the faces of the early church believers and many were drawn to Him as a result.

The church of today, filled with the Holy Spirit, will illuminate the love and charity of Jesus Christ to their local neighborhoods and communities resulting in a new hunger for the gospel. They will literally earn the right to be heard and their message of love backed by actions will be powerful. *"And the* LORD *was adding to their number day by day those who were being saved"* (Acts 2:47). We too will see people saved and added to the Kingdom as God does His marvelous work in and through us.

Application:

Pentecost, the birth of the church, was an exciting time. The early church experienced the filling of the Holy Spirit and God moved in a tremendous way. Miracles were being done and lives were changed; people were healed and set free from sin. Souls were saved by the outreach of believers showing forth the love of Christ. The good news of the gospel of Jesus Christ was proclaimed throughout Jerusalem, then to Judea, and into the country of Samaria, and then to the outer most parts of the world. The believers were obedient to the heavenly calling, and they spread the message of God's love to a lost world. And there was a sense of awe as God continued to do miracles through the hands of the apostles. God can do the same today and we can experience another Pentecost. I believe God wants to again empower His church with the filling of the Holy Spirit. We can see the fire of God fall once more if we will ask in faith. Jesus said, *"If you then, being evil, know how to give good gifts to your children, how much more shall your heavenly Father give the Holy Spirit to those who ask Him"* (Luke 11:13)? The anointing, the fresh filling of the Holy Spirit, is there for all of us. Wanted! God to pure out on us a fresh filling of the Holy Spirit. This is the purpose of seasons of refreshing from the presence of the LORD.

In closing this chapter, I am reminded of an old hymn by Elwod H. Stokes, entitled *Fill Me Now*. May his lyrics be our prayer.

Hover o'er me, Holy Spirit, bathe my trembling heart and brow;
Fill me with Thy hallowed presence, Come, O come and fill me now.

Fill me now, fill me now, Jesus, come and fill me now;
Fill me with Thy hallowed presence, Come, O come and fill me now.

Thou canst fill me, gracious Spirit, Though I cannot tell Thee how;
But I need Thee, greatly need Thee, Come, O come and fill me now.

Fill me now, fill me now, Jesus, come and fill me now;
Fill me with Thy hallowed presence, Come, O come and fill me
now.

I am weakness, full of weakness, At Thy sacred feet I bow;
Blest, divine, eternal Spirit, Fill with pow'r and fill me now.

Fill me now, fill me now, Jesus, come and fill me now;
Fill me with Thy hallowed presence, Come, O come and fill me
now

Cleanse and comfort, bless and save me, Bathe, O bathe my
heart and brow; Thou art comforting and saving, Thou art
sweetly filling now.

Fill me now, fill me now, Jesus, come and fill me now;
Fill me with Thy hallowed presence, Come, O come and fill me
now. (18)

Recall & Application:

1. How did Pentecost affect the Disciples?

_____

_____

2. What was Peter like before and after he was filled with the Holy Spirit?

_____

_____

3. Why did the people have a sense of "awe" at what was taking place through the Apostles?

_____

_____

4. What did the Disciples and others devote themselves to after Pentecost?

_____

_____

5. Do you desire to experience another Pentecost? If so, what do you think is hindering a move of God in your life?

_____

_____

6. When God speaks, do I listen? God spoke to me in the following ways:

_____

_____

Applying Part Two
The Direction to Seasons of Refreshing:

Applying what we have learned.

Journeying through this book, we have looked at the desperation for seasons of refreshing. Our nation is in need of revival, a moving of God in restoring righteousness. Our communities are in need of revival, a moving of God in restoring truth and justice. Our churches are in need of revival, a moving of God in restoring holy living. Our homes are in need of revival, a moving of God in restoring Biblical relationships and role models. And we, as individuals, are in need of revival—a moving of God to fill us again with the Holy Spirit.

We close this section with a plea that God would take what we have read and apply it to our lives. May we be willing to come unto Jesus and surrender our burdens and cares, and in turn take His Yoke and learn of Him. May we have a fresh vision of who God is, so that we can see ourselves for what we are, in desperate need of our Savior. And may we once again experience the fresh anointing of the Holy Spirit as in the day of Pentecost. God grant us seasons of refreshing from the presence of the LORD. *"O God, grant us another Pentecost, for our nation, our communities, our churches, our homes, and we, are in so great a need for it. In Jesus name! Amen."*

Part Three: The Determination for Seasons of Refreshing.

1. The decision reached. **2.** Firmness of purpose; resolve. **3.** Resolution.

My heart is fixed, O God, my heart is fixed: I will sing and give praise. (Psalm 57:7)

He who is steadfast in righteousness will attain to life, And he who pursues evil will bring about his own death. (Proverbs 11:19)

Therefore, my beloved brethren, be steadfast, immovable, always abounding in the work of the LORD, knowing that your toil is not in vain in the LORD. (1 Corinthians 15:57)

"Therefore we also, since we are surrounded by so great a cloud of witnesses, let us lay aside every weight, and the sin which so easily ensnares us, and let us run with endurance the race that is set before us, ²looking unto Jesus, the author and finisher of our faith, who for the joy that was set before Him endured the cross, despising the shame, and has sat down at the right hand of the throne of God." (Hebrews 12:1-2)

I am resolved no longer to linger, Charmed by the world's delight;
Things that are higher, things that are nobler, These have allured my sight.
I will hasten to Him, Hasten so glad and free;
Jesus, Greatest, Highest, I will come to Thee.
(I Am Resolved, by Palmer Hartsough)

Therefore, gird your minds for action, keep sober in spirit, fix your hope completely on the grace to be brought to you at the revelation of Jesus Christ. As obedient children, do not be conformed to the former lusts which were yours in your ignorance, but like the Holy One who called you, be holy yourselves also in all your behavior; because it is written, "YOU SHALL BE HOLY, FOR I AM HOLY."

And if you address as Father the One who impartially judges according to each man's work, conduct yourselves in fear during the time of your stay upon earth; knowing that you were not redeemed with perishable things like silver or gold from your futile way of life inherited from your forefathers, but with precious blood, as of a lamb unblemished and spotless, the blood of Christ.

For He was foreknown before the foundation of the world, but has appeared in these last times for the sake of you who through Him are believers in God, who raised Him from the dead and gave Him glory, so that your faith and hope are in God. Since you have in obedience to the truth purified your souls for a sincere love of the brethren, fervently love one another from the heart, for you have been born again not of seed which is perishable but imperishable, that is, through the living and abiding word of God. (1 Peter 1:13-23)

Chapter 8

Overcoming the Hindrances to Seasons of Refreshing

Keeping the Times of Refreshing:

God delights in our Fellowship:

When a person experiences a personal revival with God, the question often asked is, *"How does one continue to develop an intimate relationship with Jesus Christ?"* In answering this, it is important to first look at the hindrances to experiencing seasons of refreshing. Let's begin with understanding that God desires our fellowship far more than we can comprehend or understand. God has gone, and will continue to go to great lengths in order to draw us near to Him and experience His refreshing. God delights in meeting with His people. He is there in our time of need, He is there when we pray, and He is there when we rejoice in worship. He wants to be a part of our lives, in times of leisure as well as in times of trial. He is our Heavenly Father who is near and not distant or indifferent. Knowing and applying this to our lives will bring a new sense of peace.

God delights in our fellowship! Sounds strange, but it is true! God wants to be a part of our desires and concerns. He cares about those details in our lives that we think no one else does. He wants to be intimately involved in our decision-making and He wants us to trust Him with the results. He listens to our prayers and even helps us to pray when we are to burdened. He is our "Abba Father," our "Daddy, Daddy," the one who loves us unconditionally, immeasurably, and immensely.

We grieve our heavenly Father by sinning and rebelling against His commands. When we refuse to acknowledge sin, our fellowship with Him is hindered. His presence seems distant—we no longer experience times of refreshing. To continue in sin will only produce a hardness of heart and insensitivity toward the Holy Spirit. We will no longer hear the still, small voice of God calling us back to Him. These hindrances break our times of refreshing from the presence of the LORD. The Apostle John warned us about three categories, which are the lusts of the flesh, the lusts of the eyes, and the pride of life. Let's examine these hindrances more closely and see how they affect our fellowship with our LORD.

The Hindrances:

"As obedient children, do not be conformed to the former lusts which were yours in your ignorance," (1 Peter 2:14)

The former lusts, meaning that which was in the past and should not now be part of our lifestyle! These past lusts have been forgiven and washed by the blood of the Lamb. By faith in Jesus Christ, He has cleansed us and made us righteous in His sight. Therefore, we are a new creation in Christ and the former sins are no longer a problem, right? Wrong! As long as we have breath, we will face "the former lusts." The command is, don't be conformed to them, literally, don't give in to or be controlled by them. So, as we examine these former lusts, let's make sure that they are no longer in control.

I. The Lusts of the Flesh. (1 John 2:16)

The lusts of the flesh, literally the cravings of sinful men, are expressed in a selfish, self-centered lifestyle. It is a desire to please self at any cost. The cry of the world is, *"If it feels good, do it!"* The consequences don't matter as long as it feels good for the moment. In contrast, Paul warns, *"Do nothing from selfishness or empty conceit, but with humility of mind let each of you regard one another as more important than himself; do not merely look out for your own personal interests, but also for the interests of others"* (Phil 2:3-4). The lusts, or the cravings of sinful men, always look to satisfying or pleasing self. But the one who desires to please God will look at or desire to meet the needs of others.

An example of the "cravings of sinful man" can be found in the book of Genesis chapter three, when Eve was being tempted by the serpent to eat of the forbidden fruit. In this chapter we read, *"when the woman saw that the tree was good for food..."* Seeing the fruit as something good to eat is not sinful in itself, but that is not being applied here. She was told not to eat from the tree of good and evil by God, and there were serious

179

consequences behind that warning. God had said, *"For in the day that you eat from it you shall surely die."* Yet, Eve was standing before that tree, admiring the fruit, and having a conversation with the serpent. She saw the fruit on the tree was good for food and there was a desire within her to eat that which God had expressly forbidden. She was choosing to gratify self over obedience to God, and the consequences of her action would be devastating. But Eve didn't think about the tragic results of sin, as she could only see or feel her desire for the fruit.

Similar to telling your children not to go near the street— they will come right up to the very edge. Just as telling your child not to touch the stove, they inevitably will. There is within each of us the desire to do that, which is forbidden. We want to push the limits, to see how close we can come to sin without getting burned. Many of us are no different than Eve, as we live to please self over the needs of our family or God's commands. The end results are the same, it is still sin. We call it "happy hour, social drinking." God calls it drunkenness. We say it's adult entertainment; God calls it lusts and perversion. We call it being overweight. God calls it gluttony. We call it an alternative lifestyle. God calls it homosexuality and an abomination. These are the lust of the flesh, which appeals to the physical desires of man and must be controlled by the Spirit. If it is not kept in check or under control, the lusts of the flesh, (the cravings of sinful man) will destroy one's purity.

II. The Lusts of the Eyes. (1 John 2:16)

"The lusts of the eyes" is the awakening of the covetous nature within our flesh. The world would say, *"I want what I want no matter what."* It is made up of greed, sexual passion, materialism, etc. It is represented in the actions and attitudes of an individual seeking to satisfy his emotional and physical needs at any price. In contrast the book of Colossians instructs, *"If then you have been raised up with Christ, keep seeking the things above, where Christ is, seated at the right hand of God. Set your mind on the things above, not on the things that are on earth"* (Col 3:1-2). The person who seeks after the lusts of the eyes will set his desire on that which gives him pleasure for the moment. The Godly person will set his affections on heaven and seek to please the One who has redeemed him. In Genesis, chapter three, Eve had just seen the tree was good for food, now she sees, *"that it was a delight to the eyes."* She saw the forbidden fruit as desirous, something she wanted regardless of

> *Many today rationalize their sin on how it will make them feel for the moment. Whether it is power, materialism, or sexual promiscuity, it will indeed make you feel good for the moment, but OH the consequences!*

the warning from God. She was rationalizing within her heart that this fruit would be great to taste and would make her happy. Wrong!

Many today rationalize their sin on how it will make them feel for the moment. Whether it is power, materialism, or sexual promiscuity, it will indeed make you feel good for the moment, but OH the consequences! We use this rationalization to buy things we don't need, and the end result is indebtedness. We rationalize promiscuity and the end results are sexually transmitted diseases or AIDS. We rationalize our "power trips," as the drive to succeed, but the end results are broken homes and broken families. Once again we call it "an affair." God calls it adultery. We call it business savvy. God calls it greed. We call it "living the good life." God calls it worldliness. We call it getting ahead, working our way up the ladder. God calls it corruption and dishonesty. These are the lusts of the eyes, which appeal to the emotions as well as the flesh, and it must be kept in check or it will destroy our focus.

III. The Pride of Life. (1 John 2:26)

The pride of life is literally the boasting of what one has or does. It is the desire or passion to be better than someone else— a proud, arrogant heart that makes its boast in one's position in society, business, or status and wealth. It is the attitude that looks down on others as being less significant. It is a philosophy that uses people as tools in order to get ahead. It doesn't matter who is in the way or how many may get hurt in the process. The world claims, *"I am the master of my fate, I am the captain of my soul."* In other words, life revolves around me; I am a self-made man. In contrast, the Christian is commanded to, *"Humble yourselves, therefore, under the mighty hand of God, that He may exalt you at the proper time"* (1 Peter 5:5). Whereas, the worldly or fleshly man seeks to be proud and arrogant, the Godly man seeks to be clothed in humility in order to please the One who will exalt him in due time.

In Genesis, chapter three, Eve after seeing the fruit as good for food and a delight to the eyes, now notices *"that the tree was desirable to make one wise."* She desired what was forbidden—thinking it would provide her with an advantage over God. The serpent had told her she would be as God, knowing good and evil. (1) The same line of thinking, which caused Satan to fall, is now being used to entice Eve to give in to pride. *"Pride goes before destruction, And a haughty spirit*

> *These three "lusts" make up the hindrances to seasons of refreshing. The lusts of the flesh will destroy your purity. The lusts of the eyes will destroy your focus and the pride of life will destroy your character.*

before stumbling," is the wisdom in Proverbs 16:18. All pride and arrogance of heart will lead to destruction because God hates pride! (2) Once again, we call it shrewd business practices. God calls it a heart that devices wicked plans. We call it social status, a place in society. God calls it a proud look. We call it the fast track to success and wealth. God calls it feet that run rapidly to do evil. The pride of life must be kept in check, controlled by the Holy Spirit or it will destroy one's character.

These three "lusts" make up the hindrances to seasons of refreshing. The lusts of the flesh will destroy your purity. The lusts of the eyes will destroy your focus and the pride of life will destroy your character. That is why Peter said, *"Beloved, I urge you as aliens and strangers to abstain from fleshly lusts, which wage war against the soul"* (1 Peter 2:11). These lusts are constantly warring against your soul, meaning the battle is continually raging and it will never be over until we are home with Jesus. However, if we are willing to walk in the Spirit, the victory is already ours through Christ. Paul commands us to walk in the Spirit and we will not carryout the desires of the flesh. (3) When Satan tempted Jesus in the wilderness, he used the same three "lusts" he used on Eve and uses on us today. But Jesus resisted the devil with the Word of God, as an example for us to prepare ourselves the same way. The battle is real, the temptations are great, and the hindrances to seasons of refreshing are strong. However, Peter gives us a battle plan!

The Battle Plan: A Holy Life.

If we are to maintain seasons of refreshing from the presence of the LORD, we must live a holy life. Christ has given His righteousness to each believer, therefore, we are already declared holy in our position. But our walk can be unholy at times because we allow sin to reign within us. We have looked at the hindrances to seasons of refreshing and we must be prepared to wage war against those sins. The battle plan Peter describes will lead us to victory, if we are willing to apply it.

I. The Preparation for the Soldier before the Battle:

"Therefore, gird your minds for action, keep sober in spirit, fix your hope completely on the grace to be brought to you at the revelation of Jesus Christ." (1 Peter 1:13)

"Be ready, stay alert, and remain focused!" That is the solemn warning of any night commander in a battlefield situation. Be ready to react instantly in any given situation. Stay alert to the schemes or devices of the enemy and remain focused on the objective.

The believer is called to do the same, for this is part of the preparation for battle. The enemy seeks to get us sidetracked by the lusts of the flesh, the lust of the eyes, and the pride of life. He seeks to lure us to sleep by complacency and indifference. And he seeks to get our eyes off Jesus and onto the cares of this world. We must be alert to the enemy's schemes and stay focused on the objective, which is our constant fellowship with the Father.

If we anticipate, we will prepare, and if we are prepared we will be victorious. This takes tough-minded holiness, a determination to walk in obedience to the Word and the will of God.

Be Ready! Peter tells us to prepare

our minds for action; in other words, we must anticipate confronta-tions with the enemy of your soul and the struggles with your sinful nature. If we anticipate, we will prepare, and if we are prepared we will be victorious. This takes tough-minded holiness, a determination to walk in obedience to the Word and will of God. When Jesus was confronted by Satan in the wilderness, He quoted scriptures to resist the tempter's offers. (4) To prepare our minds for action involves memorizing scripture and having a working knowledge of the Bible. Having our minds prepared can be summed up in this statement, "know what you believe and believe in what you know." Having this in mind, we can resist any temptation by the Word of God. We have a scriptural basis for our resistance and can stand firm in our faith. Learning and memorizing scriptures takes time, discipline, and determination. But if we don't prepare ourselves, we will become an open target for temptation. We have seen the results of individuals giving into momentary temptations, all because they didn't prepare themselves for the coming battle. Be ready; prepare your mind for action!

Stay Alert!

Peter tells us to keep sober in spirit or to literally "be self-controlled." Remember, the fruit of the Spirit is self-control, which is to put all our desires, passions, and wants under the controlling influence of the Holy Spirit. (5) To be "sober minded" or "self-controlled," is to be free from every mental or physical excess. The believer is not controlled by outside circumstances, but is directed from within. He is not controlled by the flesh, nor has the need to fulfill the desires of the flesh, but his longing is to abide in the presence of God. In preparation for daily battles, not only does he need to be ready, but he needs to be "sober minded" or "self-controlled" as well.

Self-control involves spiritual discipline. It is applying the right scriptures at the right time to overcome temptation, discouragement, and the various trials that will come our way. I am reminded of King David's temptation with Bathsheba. (6) One evening, while David was walking on his balcony, he saw Bathsheba bathing. Right then he had to make a choice, give into the temptation, or resist it and move on. Sadly, he gave into the temptation and the results were disastrous for his family and himself. God has given us the power to resist any and all temptation with the filling of the Holy Spirit and the Word of God. Remember when Jesus was tempted in the wilderness to turn the stones into bread, He responded by quoting from the Torah, Deuteronomy 8:3, *"Man shall not live by bread alone, but by every word that proceeds out of the mouth of God."* Jesus resisted the temptation Satan was throwing at Him by the Word of God and so can we. Our preparation for the battle is to be self-controlled!

Remain Focused!

Peter tells us to fix our hope completely on His grace and focus our attention on the soon return of our LORD Jesus Christ. The very thought of His sudden appearing should challenge every one of us to be ready, alert, and focused on Him. To live in anticipation of His return is to be ready at all times. It is to be focused on Him and not get bogged down in sin, self, and situations that will hinder our fellowship and seasons of refreshing from His presence.

To fix our hope completely, is to set our focus on Jesus Christ. It is a determination to remain fixed on the course that He has set before us. Like setting a compass, it will always point due north even in the worst of storms. We can weather the storms of life when we fix our eyes on the grace He has given us and will continue to show us. Peter had first hand knowledge about that statement. One night during a severe storm, as they were rowing their boat across the sea of Galilee, the Disciples saw Jesus walking toward them on the water. (7) The other Disciples thought they were seeing a ghost, but Peter had the courage and faith to ask Jesus to let him walk on the water as well. And he did! As long as his eyes were fixed on Jesus, Peter walked on water. Peter was doing the impossible because his eyes, his hope, and his confidence were focused on Jesus Christ, the Son of God. But when Peter took his eyes off of Jesus, and looked at the storm raging around him, he began to sink. This same lesson is applicable for us today—stay focused on Jesus! Set your confidence completely on the grace and mercy He continually gives, and anticipate His soon return.

If we are to overcome the hindrances to seasons of refreshing, we must prepare ourselves for the battle that lies before us. We can do that by being ready, staying alert, and remaining focused.

II. The Practice of the Soldier in Battle.

"As obedient children, do not be conformed to the former lusts which were yours in your ignorance, but like the Holy One who called you, be holy yourselves also in all your behavior; because it is written, "YOU SHALL BE HOLY, FOR I AM HOLY." And if you address as Father the One who impartially judges according to each man's work, conduct yourselves in fear during the time of your stay upon earth" (1 Peter 1:14-17);

We have talked about the preparation of the soldier for battle, now let's look at the practice of the soldier in battle. The focus is on conduct, and like any good soldier, discipline prevails. We, like soldiers, are in a very real battle and our King demands obedience and discipline. If we are committed to our King, His demands are not grievous but delightful. Our practice as a soldier in battle will be walking in obedience, living a holy life, and conducting ourselves in the reverential fear of our LORD.

Be Obedient!

Peter is telling us to walk in obedience and to not be conformed to the former lusts, which were ours in ignorance. We have already talked about the former lusts as part of our study on the hindrances to seasons of refreshing. Now let's look at what it means to walk in obedience.

The practice of a soldier in battle is to obey instantly, without question or hesitation. The characteristic of a good soldier is to follow orders exclusively and thoroughly which is expected and commanded. Our Commander-in-Chief would expect the same from us. The obedience of the soldier in battle may save his life and others and it may mean the difference between victory and defeat. The same is true for the believer, as God demands our instant obedience without question or hesitation. When we obey with this type of zeal, God can and will use us to His glory. Second Chronicles 16:9 states, *"The eyes of the LORD run to and fro throughout the whole earth, to show himself strong in the behalf of them whose heart is perfect toward him."* God is not looking for the high in status, the special rank, or the privilege; Rather, He is looking for someone whose heart's cry is for His presence and who has a desire to obey and serve regardless of the costs.

Obedience brings blessing, disobedience brings chastisement. This is a simple but true statement to remember. God will bless the obedient and reward the faithful, but the disobedient will face confrontation and anguish continually. Obedience is not only the external action of the believer, but the inward attitude of the heart. God wants us to obey Him from a heart of love. Jesus said to His Disciples, *"If you love Me you will keep My commandments."* (8) That statement is as true today as it was then. If we really love the Savior we will obey Him.

Peter uses the illustration of a child to convey the importance of this particular passage. As a child is asked to obey his parents instantly, thoroughly, and with the right attitude, so we too, as children of God, must do the same. When we walk in disobedience, problems arise and we often return to the "former lusts." Throughout scriptures, it is evident God blesses those who obey Him and He disciplines those who will not. Our earthly fathers did the same. When I acted in rebellion and disobedience, I usually got what I deserved and it hurt to sit down for a while. But when I obeyed, my father was pleased because it showed that I honored and respected him.

Remember the practice of the soldier in battle is to obey his commanding officer. To win over the battles of the flesh, we as soldiers, must be disciplined and obedient so that the victory will be ours.

Be Exemplary In Your Behavior!

Peter is telling us to be "holy" in all of our conduct, just as the One who called us is holy. But what does it really mean to live a holy life? To be holy is to reflect the new nature within us. That new nature is the presence and power of the Holy Spirit, which was discussed in the last chapter. Remember everyday there are "opportunities" that arise which God asks us to trust Him and to yield to His Lordship. Part of that process is yielding to the controlling influence of the Holy Spirit. When faced with temptation—desiring to respond in the flesh—God is still asking us to trust Him and yield to the Holy Spirit's control. And if we are obedient children, we will.

Though absolute holiness can never be achieved in this life, all areas of our life should be in the process of becoming completely conformed to God's perfect and holy will. Everyday our desire and walk should become more like Jesus. When we fail, and we will, we have the provision of 1 John 1:9 that, *"If we confess our sins, He is faithful and righteous to forgive us our sins and to cleanse us from all unrighteousness."* We can walk in holiness because God has given us the Holy Spirit to strengthen and empower us. We can maintain a holy attitude because God has given us His Word to mediate on and apply to our lives. We can live in holiness because God has given us the provision of 1 John 1:9.

The practice of a good soldier in battle is to live a disciplined life. Too many soldiers have let down their guard during leave and compromised their morality only to pay a dire price. Many believers have done the same in their walk. A holy, disciplined life would have saved many from the heartache and tragic consequences of their actions. Be holy is a command by the One who demands obedience and it is for our own good that we should follow His commands.

Fear the Consequences!

Peter is telling the believer to live as a stranger in reverent fear. The practice of a soldier in battle not only involved obedience and a discipline life, but a reverent fear of the consequences. He knows the tragic results if he fails, he may be brave but he is not a fool! Therefore, he respects his enemy, the territory he is in, and the combat situation he faces. The believer in Christ should have the same reverent fear toward the LORD that he serves, the enemy he faces, and the territory he is in.

To have a reverent fear toward the LORD is to realize His holiness and righteousness is beyond our comprehension. Therefore, we show the proper respect in our actions and attitudes when we approach Him in prayer, worship, or praise. We have a desire to live a life pleasing to Him and a willingness to walk in obedience. Remember we are strangers or literally, "aliens" in the land. There is also a "fear" in living a life of disobedience because as a Father, He will discipline His children.

The believer must also have a reverent fear for the "real enemy" he faces—not to run in terror or be afraid—but to have a respect for the power that the devil has. To respect that power is to understand, in our own strength, we cannot resist his temptations. It is to be aware of the schemes the devil will use to trip us up and to be prepared for those schemes. It is to understand Satan is looking for a "toehold" in our life that will turn into a "beachhead," so we must take the necessary steps to shore up our defenses.

Just as the soldier has a reverent fear for the territory he is in, so too must the believer. He must realize he is a stranger in a foreign land, this is not his home! Therefore, he must keep himself free from entanglements that will distract him of his mission.

This is the practice of the soldier in the battle, he is obedient, disciplined, and he has a reverent fear or respect for the enemy he faces. The practice of the believer in battle is to walk obediently, live a holy lifestyle, and conduct oneself in reverent fear towards his LORD and the battle he faces.

III.   The Position of the Soldier through the Battle:

"Knowing that you were not redeemed with perishable things like silver or gold from your futile way of life inherited from your forefathers, but with precious blood, as of a lamb unblemished and spotless, the blood of Christ. For you have been born again, not of perishable seed, but of imperishable, through the living and enduring word of God. For, "All men are like grass, and all their glory is like the flowers of the field; the grass withers and the flowers fall, but the word of the LORD stands forever." And this is the word that was preached to you." (1 Peter 1:18-19, 23-25)

We have looked at the preparation of the soldier for the battle; he was to be ready, to stay alert and remain focused. We have also looked at the practice of the soldier in battle, he was to be obedient, disciplined, and conduct himself in fear during his stay or tour of duty. Now let's look at the position of the soldier through the battle.

They say positioning is everything! To the soldier, it could mean having the strategic advantage of high ground, or cover, or the ability to mobilize quickly. To the believer his positioning is knowing who he is and the price of his redemption. Understanding this will strengthen our position through the battle we face continually and will lead us to ultimate victory in Christ.

Remember the Price Paid!

Peter tells us of the high price that was paid for our redemption. It wasn't gold, silver, or precious stones, because those things perish. But it was the precious blood of the Lamb of God. Jesus willingly gave Himself to purchase sinful man from the slave market of sin and death. The price of our redemption, the precious blood of the Lamb, should give us an idea of our position in Christ. The Apostle Paul tells us we are children of God and fellow heirs with Christ. (9) Our position is one of a relationship, we are sons and therefore joint heirs with Christ and our inheritance is waiting in heaven for us. This should give us courage through the battles we're in and motivate us to live holy lives.

Understanding the believer's position in Christ will give us hope and confidence in any situation. When we are tempted, this should be our motivating factor to resist sin. When we face attacks from the enemy, this should be the weapon of our warfare and when we become discouraged, this should be our source of strength. Knowing Jesus loved us enough to shed His blood in order to redeem and give us eternal life, will be the source of our power!

Our inheritance in Christ, Peter told us, *"is imperishable and undefiled and will not fade away, reserved in heaven for you."* (10) Our position in Christ is secured, we are forever His and He is forever ours. This is our joy and our sure victory!

Jesus Christ paid the price of our redemption so that we might walk in newness of life and He has provided everything we need to live in fellowship with Him. Therefore, let us remember the price of our redemption and seek to please the One who has called us into this fellowship. Let us remember our position through this battle is one of "sonship," we are the children of the living God!

Abide in the Word of God.

Peter tells us the grass withers and the flowers fall off but the Word of the LORD abides forever. If God's Word is forever, shouldn't that be incentive enough to read it? To abide in God's

Word is to spend time studying and researching it, to seek the wisdom of the Holy Spirit in order to open truth and apply it to our lives. If the believer is to remain victorious through the battle, he must put on the sword of the Spirit, which is the Word of God. (11)

A soldier would spend time studying his enemy, learning his strengths and weaknesses. He would spend time studying the battle plan to overcome the enemy and to prepare for the assault. He would know the orders of his commander and prepare to carry them out fully. And he would position himself to insure that the outcome would be victorious.

Our position in this battle we call life, is like a diligent soldier who faithfully "studies to show himself approved unto God, as one who doesn't need to be ashamed, rightly dividing the word of truth." (12) Like a diligent soldier, we prepare for the assault of the enemy by studying the battle plans of our Commander as we willingly carry out His orders.

This is the position of the soldier throughout the battle, knowing who he is and where his authority lies, and he is diligently studying the battle plan, prepared to carry out all orders given.

Application: The Power of a Holy Life.

We have looked at the hindrances to seasons of refreshing made up of the continual struggles of the lusts of the flesh, the lusts of the eyes, and the boastful pride of life. These hindrances we face daily. They can creep in subtly and if not detected, can rob us of our intimacy with God.

We looked at the battle plan to overcome those hindrances and we compared them to a soldier preparing for battle, a soldier's practice in the battle, and a soldier's position throughout the battle.

If we are to maintain an intimacy with God, to daily experience seasons of refreshing from His presence, we must have a holy walk. Sin cannot reign in our lives. We must be obedient children and not be conformed to the former lusts that were once ours. A holy life is a life lived in obedience to the Word and will of God. It is staying focused on the mission God has called us to, and to faithfully serve Him. A holy life is to remember the price of our redemption; it wasn't paid by silver or gold, but by the precious blood of the Lamb of God. Remember that a holy life is to faithfully abide in the Word of God and to diligently study and apply what has been learned.

I. A Holy Life is a Powerful Life in Prayer.

Consider this verse from the book of James, *"The effectual fervent prayer of a righteous man availeth much"* (James 5:16). Prayer is effectual when it is backed by a holy lifestyle. The fervent prayer of a righteous man accomplishes much, because he is righteous. Righteousness comes from Jesus Christ giving His righteousness to us by faith. We have been declared righteous in God's eyes by the blood of Jesus Christ. However, our walk must be righteous by being obedient to the Word of God. When you put a holy lifestyle and Christ's righteousness together, prayer becomes effective and it accomplishes much. If we want to see our prayers answered, if we desire to see God move powerfully in and through our lives, a holy life becomes a necessity. The Psalmist David said, *"If I regard iniquity in my heart, the LORD will not hear me."* (13) David knew to hide sin would hinder his prayer life, his fellowship, and literally his season of refreshing from the presence of the LORD. But in the next verse he said, *"But verily God hath heard me; he hath attended to the voice of my prayer."* (14) Why did God hear him and attend to his prayer? Because he did not regard or hide sin, rather he repented of it.

II. A Holy Life is a Powerful Life in Practice.

For the true businessperson, his affairs are done above board. There are no under-the-table contracts, shady practices, or unethical dealings. To the true employee, he or she is honest, hard working, and doesn't murmur or complain. The results of this type of lifestyle will shock an unbelieving world because it brings conviction on the ones who are unethical, immoral, or dishonest. Scriptures are full of examples of men and women who wouldn't compromise their integrity. Daniel was an example of such integrity because he was cast into the lion's den for practicing a holy lifestyle of praying three times daily. Scriptures record that Daniel's enemies could find no ground of accusation, or evidence of corruption, or negligence in regard to governmental affairs. His enemies openly admitted, *"We shall not find any ground of accusation against this Daniel unless we find it against him with regard to the law of his God."* (15) Daniel put into practice a holy lifestyle and God blessed and honored him for it.

III.   A Holy Life is a Powerful Life in Principle.

A holy lifestyle is staying faithful to what is true and right. It is living an uncompromising life that will not be bought, seduced, or corrupted. Again, scriptures are full of men and women who lived holy lives based on Godly principles. Joseph, is an example of one who lived a holy life even when tempted day after day by Potiphar's wife to seduce her. Scriptures record he steadfastly refused saying, *"How can I do this great evil, and sin against God?"* (16) He chose to live a holy life in spite of the pressure to

> *Doctrine determines lifestyle! If our doctrine is based on Biblical principles of holy living, we will practice what we believe.*

compromise his integrity. Because of his character, God honored Joseph. Throughout Joseph's trials, from Potiphar's house to prison to Pharaoh's court—you see Joseph living a holy life. He was faithful and true to the principles, God had taught him.

Doctrine determines lifestyle! If our doctrine is based on Biblical principles of holy living, we will practice what we believe; resulting in a powerful lifestyle God can use to witness to an unbelieving world. However, if our doctrine is based on compromise, our integrity will be lacking and we will live inconsistent lives.

In maintaining seasons of refreshing—keeping intimacy with God, means living a holy life. On occasion, we do fail because our sinful nature sometimes gets the best of us. However, we have the assurance if we confess our sin, He is faithful and just to forgive us of our sin and cleanse us from all unrighteousness (1 John 1:9). If we are willing to keep our Christian bar of soap handy, and use it, we can continue to develop that intimacy with our loving heavenly Father.

In closing of this chapter, let us look at the words of the old hymn "*More Holiness Give Me,* by Philip P. Bliss and let these words speak to your heart.

More holiness give me, More striving within;
More patience in suffering, More sorrow for sin;
More faith in my Savior, More sense of His care;
More joy in His service, More purpose in prayer.

More gratitude give me, More trust in the LORD;
More patience in suffering, More sorrow for sin;
More tears for His sorrows, More pain at His grief;
More meekness in trials, More praise for relief.

More purity give me, More strength to o'ercome;
More freedom from earth-stains, More longings for
home;
More fit for the kingdom, More used would I be;
More blessed and holy, More, Savior, like Thee. (17)

Recall & Application

1. What are the three hindrances to maintaining times of refreshing?

    _____

    _____

2. What are the three preparations for the soldier before the battle?

    _____

    _____

3. What three practices were mentioned for the soldier in the battle?

    _____

    _____

4. A "holy life" is powerful in what three ways?

    _____

    _____

5. If I am to maintain seasons of refreshing from the presence of the LORD, I must practice 1 John 1:9, which says...

    _____

    _____

6. When God speaks, do I listen? God spoke to me in the following ways:

    _____

    _____

And He said to them, "Suppose one of you shall have a friend, and shall go to him at midnight, and say to him, 'Friend, lend me three loaves; for a friend of mine has come to me from a journey, and I have nothing to set before him'; and from inside he shall answer and say, 'Do not bother me; the door has already been shut and my children and I are in bed; I cannot get up and give you anything.''"

"I tell you, even though he will not get up and give him anything because he is his friend, yet because of his persistence he will get up and give him as much as he needs."
"And I say to you, ask, and it shall be given to you; seek, and you shall find; knock, and it shall be opened to you. "For everyone who asks, receives; and he who seeks, finds; and to him who knocks, it shall be opened.

"Now suppose one of you fathers is asked by his son for a fish; he will not give him a snake instead of a fish, will he? "Or if he is asked for an egg, he will not give him a scorpion, will he? "If you then, being evil, know how to give good gifts to your children, how much more shall your heavenly Father give the Holy Spirit to those who ask Him?"
(Luke 11:5-13)

Chapter 9

The Granting of Seasons of Refreshing:
Persistency in Prayer

It was a warm September day in metropolitan New York as a quiet, zealous businessman named Jeremiah Lanphier made his way to the North Dutch Reformed Church on Fulton Street. He had been appointed as the new city missionary with the charge of recruiting people to attend their fellowship and come to know Christ as their Savior. The North Dutch Reform Church had been suffering from a depletion of membership due in part to the removal of the population from downtown to better residential quarters. Getting the unbelievers to attend would be a challenge, for downtown neighborhoods were often in the throws of poverty and crime. Yet, Jeremiah was burdened by the need and compelled to pray. He began to solicit responses for a prayer meeting, which would start at noon on Wednesdays and last approximately one hour. He distributed handbills throughout offices and warehouses in the community, which read:

How Often Shall I Pray?
As often as the language of prayer is in my heart; as
Often as I see my need of help; as often as I feel the
Power of temptation; as often as I am made sensible
Of any spiritual declension or feel the aggression of a

worldly spirit. In prayer we leave the business of time
for that of eternity, and intercourse with men for
intercourse with God.

Lanphier announced, on the other side of the bill, that the
meeting was intended to give merchants, mechanics, clerks,
strangers, and businessmen an opportunity to stop and call
upon God amid their perplexities of the day. Though it was
planned to last for an hour, it was designed for those who could
only afford to spend ten to fifteen minutes as well.

It was noon on the 23rd of September 1857, when Jeremiah
opened the door to the North Dutch Reformed Church to begin
his prayer vigil. Alone at first, he began to call upon God to
cleanse him of sin and remove that which hinders the work of
Christ in his life. Thirty minutes later, six other businessmen
joined him and began to pray. Each one was seeking God to do
a work in and through their own lives first, then in the lives of
those in their community and ultimately the nation.

The attendance at their prayer meeting began to grow until
the first week in October 1857, when it was decided to meet
daily instead of weekly. In that same week, God began to move
in an extraordinary revival that swept over Hamilton and into
faraway Canada. In the second week of October, the great
financial panic of that year reached a crisis and flattened
business everywhere. God was shaking the foundations of
society with an economic downturn and He was pouring out
His grace on the church, calling His bride back to Him.

Within six months, ten thousand businessmen were gathering daily for prayer in New York. Within two years, a million converts were added to the American churches. Every part of the nation was touched by the prayer revival of 1857-1858. Not only was the population of the United States involved, but during these two years, this great awakening moved the people of the United Kingdom, Ulster, Scotland, Wales, and England. (1)

In the New Year of 1858, New York was beginning to see a down pouring of Divine blessing throughout the city. In February, the secular press, noticing something unprecedented was happening, began to give space to revival news. A New York daily newspaper gave widespread publicity to the movement in an editorial; it told of the crowds at the North Dutch Reformed Church on Fulton Street. (2)

At Fulton Street, the sponsors were trying to accommodate the crowds by holding three simultaneous prayer meetings in the same building. The seats were all filled and the hallways were so crowded that it was impossible for people to pass in or out. God was moving in a tremendous way within His people calling them back to prayer and repentance. There was no fanaticism or hysteria; it was simply an incredible movement of the people to pray.

On March 17, Burton's Theatre on Chambers Street in Brooklyn opened their doors for noonday prayer service. Every available space was taken a half-hour before the service begin at the theatre. Even the entrances and the street before the theatre were crowded with people desiring to pray and meet with God.

The noonday prayer meetings soon flowed over into weeknight services, with multitudes being saved and coming into the Kingdom. Before too long, over ten thousand New Yorkers had been saved and were in the care of the local church for discipleship. The national press started to carry more stories about the great awakening and the prayer movement was challenging people everywhere across the country.

The great awakening started to spread out from the Middle Atlantic States, first northward to New England, then to the south as far as Texas and westward along the Ohio valley. Every denomination was affected with new growth by the increase of conversions. A Baptist journal had reported that over 17,000 converts had taken place since the awakening began. (3) In May of 1858, an editor in New York collected interdenominational figures from as many sources as possible and showed 96,216 people had been converted and added to their churches in just recent months. (4)

The number of conversions reported to have reached fifty thousand a week during the height of the great awakening. For a period of two years, there were ten thousand additions to church membership weekly. (5)

The influence of the Revival was felt everywhere in the nation. It first captured the great metropolitan cities, than it spread through every town and village. It also affected every school, college, and learning institution in the country as God seemed to invade the nation with another Pentecost. Many predominate colleges initiated prayer services and began to see students converted to the LORD Jesus Christ. Harvard, Yale, and Oberlin College all reported conversions. Princeton, Davidson, Oglethorpe, Denison, Miami of Ohio, Berkeley, Amherst, North Carolina, Wake Forest, and Trinity all reported conversions and a new desire to learn more of Christ. (6)

In the eastern states, Boston began to experience the outpouring of Divine grace. By March of 1858, prayer meetings were springing up all over the city. All were crowded and solemn with whole assemblies often in tears as God was melting hearts and changing lives. In New Bedford, one in twenty of the people had made professions of faith. Throughout the state of Massachusetts, over one hundred and fifty towns were moved by this revival with over five thousand converted to Christ before the end of March. (7)

In Portland, Maine, great crowds gathered at the morning, noon, afternoon, and evening prayer meetings with the church bells daily summoning thousands to prayer. An extensive revival arose in Bangor and spread throughout the nearby towns; the state of Maine was experiencing seasons of refreshing leading many to salvation.

In the State of Connecticut, the revival swept through communities in an unprecedented way. Many churches were filled to capacity for the 8 a.m. prayer meeting and repeating again at 5 p.m. In several areas, businesses were closed down between 4 and 5 p.m. so that time would be given for all to pray.

In the Midwest—by April—Lexington, Covington, Frankfort, and other Kentucky towns began to experience the outpouring of revival. In the State of Ohio, two hundred towns reported as much as 12,000 conversions in a couple of months. In Indiana, a hundred and fifty towns reported from four to five thousand converts in two months of the revival. (8) From Wisconsin, to Minnesota, to Illinois, and Iowa, revival broke out with thousands coming to know Christ as Savior, lives being changed, and people desiring to pray and meet with God.

The revival of 1858, though born by prayer, was fueled by the preaching of the Word of God. Many of men were called into the ministry, and others were filled with power from on high to proclaim the truths of scripture with new boldness. Though many remained unknown and silent, yet a few would have worldwide influence. Those were the likes of D. L. Moody, William Taylor, William Booth, Hudson Taylor, C. H. Spurgeon, Charles G. Finney, and the list could go on as many were used mightily by God.

The great awakening of 1858 produced new missions and missionaries that reached unto the ends of the earth. Among those having their roots in the 1858 revival were the China Inland Mission founded by Hudson Taylor.

The true results of the 1858 great awakening will probably not be known until heaven reveals it. However, over two million souls were converted to the LORD Jesus Christ. Evangelic ministries were born and many were called to fulfill the great commission at home and abroad. Individual lives were changed, marriages restored, sins confessed and forsaken as many pursued a holy walk with Christ. Society as a whole was changed as the great awakening gave birth to new social programs that looked after the welfare of children, brought help for the alcoholic, and hope for the downtrodden. America has not experienced a revival like this since.

> *The key to the revival of 1858 was prayer—earnest, heart-felt, agonizing, persistent, and purposeful prayer.*

The key to the revival of 1858 was prayer—earnest, heart-felt, agonizing, persistent, and purposeful prayer. James tells us the effectual, fervent prayer of a righteous man accomplishes much (James 5:16). Little did Jeremiah Lanphier realize that when he began to pray and seek after God, his prayers would lead to such an outpouring of Divine grace. When the righteous begin to pray and cry out to God for His mercy, God begins to move in ways we cannot imagine. They were desperate to see God move in their midst during the revival of 1858. Is there that longing to see God move again? If so, we must have a heart that is persistent and purposeful in prayer, calling upon God to send revival again. What does it mean to be persistent and purposeful in prayer? Let's examine the scriptural text in Luke 11:5-13 and find out.

211

Persistent Prayer:

"And He said to them, "Suppose one of you shall have a friend, and shall go to him at midnight, and say to him, 'Friend, lend me three loaves; for a friend of mine has come to me from a journey, and I have nothing to set before him'; and from inside he shall answer and say, 'Do not bother me; the door has already been shut and my children and I are in bed; I cannot get up and give you anything.'

"I tell you, even though he will not get up and give him anything because he is his friend, yet because of his persistence he will get up and give him as much as he needs."

"And I say to you, ask, and it shall be given to you; seek, and you shall find; knock, and it shall be opened to you. "For everyone who asks, receives; and he who seeks, finds; and to him who knocks, it shall be opened."

I. Realizing the Need:

Persistence in prayer begins with realizing there is a need only God can fill. It is understanding the desperation of the circumstance, the difficulties of the time, and the hopelessness of the situation. It is realizing our hope and confidence is in God alone, and only He can bring about the answers we seek. Persistence in prayer is wrestling with God. Not that we have to arm-twist God into our line of thinking, but He wants to mold us into His will.

In Genesis Chapter 32, is the story of Jacob wrestling with "the angel of the LORD." Jacob, whose name meant, "to deceive" or "cheat," was returning to his homeland with his family when he heard his brother Esau was coming to meet him. The one he had connived out of his birthright was now leading a highly trained Calvary of over four hundred men. Jacob was terrified! That night, as he prayed for God's deliverance, a man stood before him and they wrestled until daybreak. The "man" was called the angel of the LORD, literally the pre-incarnate Christ. Jacob was seeking God's deliverance, but there were greater issues at stake than just Esau. It was reconciliation with God that was being forced upon Jacob that night. He had sinned both against God, against Esau, and against his aged father. It was these sins God desired to speak with Jacob about at this time. It was no doubt that this matter was being settled in Jacob's heart while they struggled.

Jacob had thought, like the rest of us that God was reluctant about giving His gifts and must be overcome by wrestling. Jacob was trying to connive God just like everyone else he had deceived. In verse 26 Jacob stated, *"I will not let you go unless you bless me."* But God was ready to bless Jacob whenever Jacob was willing to confess his sins and be reconciled to Him. In his wrestling, the angel of the LORD struck Jacob's hip dislocating it. Yet, Jacob still clung to his heavenly foe crying out, *"I will not let you go unless you bless me."* God wanted to give Jacob far more than just what he asked for. Jacob's plea was for God to protect his family and himself from Esau. God not only granted this, but also brought reconciliation between two brothers. God gave Jacob a meeting he would never forget, as he would be lame for the rest of his life. God also changed

Jacob's name to Israel, meaning he who strove with God and prevailed.

With the injury to his leg, God gave Jacob something that made him humble the rest of his life. It made him insignificant in his own eyes and totally dependent upon God. Jacob's weakness became his strength against his enemies and his persistence brought about God's blessing far more than he anticipated.

In our scriptural context, a friend has come to visit and it is late in the night. The person to whom the friend has come to, ventures over to another friend and asks for bread to feed this traveler for he has nothing to set before him. First of all, he saw the need. The weary traveler was his friend and he desired to provide for him that which he did not have. Secondly, he went to the only person he knew that could provide for his need. Third, he was persistent in his asking until his need was met.

Jesus was giving us an illustration of persistence. The friend kept on knocking on the door and asking for bread for his weary traveler, which came to visit. But the persistence was based upon compassion. The friend cared about his traveling companion enough to keep on asking and knocking until he received what he had asked. The persistence was also based on relationship. He knew who to go to, in order to receive what was needed. And thirdly, the persistence was based on steadfastness. He was not going to quit at the first no.

If we are to see a revival like the Great Awakening of 1858, if God is to grant us a season of refreshing from the presence of the LORD, then we must become persistent in our prayers. We must realize that there is a need for God to visit His people again in a supernatural way, calling us back to revival. The need is to see God give the "bread of life" to those who are lost and hungry and for the weary to find rest in the One who can strengthen and sustain them. Persistence in prayer will begin when we realize the need.

II. Recognizing the Provider:

He went to his friend and asked for bread. His friend was someone he knew would meet his need and would give generously. Even though it was late in the night and his friend had said no, he knew he would not be turned away.

The provider here, is the example of our LORD Jesus Christ. We often ask "bread" for the lost, the sick, or the needy, and it seems as if Jesus has said "No" or has remained silent. Yet, we know scriptures have said God would have all men saved and come unto the knowledge of the truth. We also know God wants to pour His Spirit out on all men and those who are weary and heavy-laden He desires to provide rest. Therefore, knowing God's will, we continue to be persistent in prayer. Because the Provider cares far more for the needs of those we are petitioning Him for than we realize. His silence or refusal at first may just be a test to see if we are going to be persistent in our prayer and compassionate in our pleading.

Jesus is our provider and the only one we can go to and ask, "bread" for those in need. We, in our own strength, cannot provide the "bread" the spiritually hungry are looking for. But when we yield to the Holy Spirit and become persistent in prayer, God can use us to bring spiritual food to the destitute. When we recognize who the provider is and how He is willing and able to provide, we can pray with boldness and assurance.

There are, and will be times when we don't know how to pray for an individual, a situation, or circumstance in which we are in. Yet we know who our provider is, and we can come to Him in our weakness and persistently seek His will to be done. And we have the assurance He will indeed provide and make known His will to us.

Again, if we are to experience another great awakening similar to what God did in 1858, it will take persistence in prayer—not only realizing the need, but recognizing who the provider is. Our hope for revival, our desire to experience seasons of refreshing from the presence of the LORD, will come when we earnestly seek the One who will provide.

Persistence in prayer not only involves realizing the need and recognizing the provider, but remaining steadfast as well.

III. Remaining Steadfast:

The friend with the weary traveler would not be turned away from his neighbor when he asked for bread. He remained steadfast even though he heard the excuses; 1) the door has been shut. 2) My children and I are in bed. 3) I cannot get up and give to you. He kept right on knocking on the door and asking until his neighbor finally gave in. Was it because of his friend's persistence and need, or was it because of annoyance and wanting to get back to sleep that he didn't give up? Either way, it produced the desired results.

God is not like that. He doesn't have to be constantly annoyed in order to grant the request of His children. However, He does want to see steadfast persistence because that will produce a compassionate heart. God wants us to be broken over the things that break His heart. He pleads with us to wrestle against the forces of darkness, knowing that the gain of man's soul or its loss is at stake. Remaining steadfast in prayer is joining with the heart of God until His will becomes ours.

God often wants to do far more for us than we realize or ask in our prayers. Martin Luther often repeated we are content to pray for silver when God wants to give us gold. The Apostle Paul best summed it up, *"Now to Him who is able to do exceeding abundantly beyond all that we ask or think"* (Eph 3:20). God wants to do the *"exceedingly abundantly above"* all we ask for in prayer, if we will remain steadfast, persistent, and not willing to give in or up.

In Matthew 15, a Canaanite woman came to Jesus to ask for the deliverance of her daughter. *"Have mercy on me, O LORD, Son of David; my daughter is cruelly demon-possessed,"* she cried out. However, Jesus didn't answer, His response was just silence. But she kept on asking or literally pleading until the Disciples began to ask Jesus to send her away. Suddenly He responded with this statement, *"I was sent only to the lost sheep of the house of Israel."* The Jews despised Canaanite's and this comment reminded her of that. Yet she would not be distracted. Then she came and fell at His feet and cried out, *"LORD, help me."* This time Jesus responded with, *"It is not good to take the children's bread and throw it to the dogs."* This was another slap at her nationality as she was being called a gentile dog. But she quickly to responded, *"Yes, LORD; but even the dogs feed on the crumbs which fall from their masters' table."* Then Jesus answered and said to her, *"O woman, your faith is great; be it done for you as you wish."* And her daughter was healed at once!

Jesus, in remaining silent and then responding harshly, was not being cruel or insensitive to her requests. Rather, He was positioning Himself to give her far more than what she was asking for her daughter. He wanted to change her life forever! At first, neither His silence nor His words offended her for she knew of her condition. Then she threw herself at His feet and surrendered to His mercy with the heart felt cry of, *"LORD, help me!"* There, at is feet, she is willing and eager to accept even the crumbs that would fall from the Master's table. Faith, humility, persistence, and steadfastness brought about the answer to her prayer and much more, a changed heart forever.

Remaining steadfast is to keep on asking and God will give you your heart's desire. Keep on seeking, God will grant mercy and grace to help in time of need. Keep on knocking, God will open wide the doors of His love.

Persistence in prayer then involves realizing the need, recognizing the provider, and remaining steadfast. However, prayer involves another aspect, and that is being "purposeful," to have a determination or a goal in mind. Jesus gave us an example of that goal in Luke 5:11-13, with the giving of the Holy Spirit.

Purposeful Prayer:

"Now suppose one of you fathers is asked by his son for a fish; he will not give him a snake instead of a fish, will he? "Or if he is asked for an egg, he will not give him a scorpion, will he? "If you then, being evil, know how to give good gifts to your children, how much more shall your heavenly Father give the Holy Spirit to those who ask Him?"

I. The Giving of the Holy Spirit:

Jesus used the illustration of a father giving good gifts to his son and then asked how much more shall your heavenly Father give the Holy Spirit to those who ask. The Holy Spirit was indeed given to believers at Pentecost and now abides in us forever, just as Jesus promised. (9) We have been sealed with the

Holy Spirit as a down payment for our future redemption, and Paul urges us to be continually filled with the Holy Spirit. But just as the illustration of a father giving good gifts to his children, so our heavenly Father wants to give us the precious gift of the outpouring of His Spirit in miraculous ways in these last days.

To be purposeful in prayer is to have a heart's cry for the outpouring of the Holy Spirit in our lives. It is a determination

> *We have not seen the hand of God move in our midst because we have not sought it. We have not experienced true worship in His presence because we do not desire it, and we have not known the power of the Holy Spirit in our lives because we have not longed for it.*

to see and experience revival, first within our own hearts and then in our churches, communities, and ultimately our nation. Jeremiah Lanphier was purposeful in his prayer as he began to call upon God to send an awakening, first into his own life, then into the life of his church. His one desire was revival and he would continue to pray in earnest until God responded with showers of blessing. Our cry today must be as his was, *"God send an awakening, revive us again and fill us with power from on high."*

To be purposeful in prayer is to have a determination to see God glorified and honored through worship, which can only be accomplished when the Holy Spirit again moves on the hearts of His people. We have not seen the hand of God move in our midst because we have not sought it. We have not experienced true worship in His presence because we do not desire it, and we have not known the power of the Holy Spirit in our lives because we have not longed for it.

Jesus promised to send the Holy Spirit to those who would ask, and if there ever was a time for asking, it is now! We are a desperate people living in desperate times with a desperate need for a fresh moving of God. The Middle East stands on the brink of war, which will surely involve the United States and possibly the rest of the world. Our cities are crime ridden, our schools are full of violence, and our churches have made no visible impact on stopping that growth or turning back the tide. The only hope America has, is the uniting of the church of Jesus Christ in earnest prayer asking God to send His Holy Spirit to revive us again.

The revival of 1858 was followed by America's bloodiest conflict, the Civil War. God was preparing His people for the onslaught of casualties, which would follow. Through those long and bitter war years, there was the need for spiritual comfort, hope, and assurance and many would look back to that great awakening and find the strength to be that witness.

Are we facing dark days ahead? Is the threat of a world war on the horizon? Then the church of Jesus Christ must prepare by seeking God to send another revival like He did in 1858. That will take earnest, heart felt, persistent prayer in order to see God move in our midst.

II. Travailing:

Being purposeful in prayer involves travailing. Travailing speaks of a woman in childbirth, the anguish of laboring to bring forth life. Rachel, in Genesis 35, travailed to bring forth her second son and died in the process. To Rachel, her travailing brought sorrow and death to herself, yet life to her child.

Hannah, in 1 Samuel 1, travailed in prayer for a son, desiring a man-child more than life itself. And like birth pangs, she labored intensely in prayer until God heard her cries. Hannah prayed if God would give her a son, she would give him back to the LORD for His service. Hannah was willing to die in order to produce life. When her son Samuel was weaned, she took him to the house of the LORD at Shilo to be raised by Eli the priest and be trained in the ministry and duties of the priesthood. She willingly gave up her desire to raise her son in order to fulfill her promise to God. God took her son and molded him into a tremendous prophet of the LORD in a time of desperation. To Hannah, giving up her son meant death to her, but life to the nation of Israel.

In both these incidences travailing brought forth life. Rachel travailed in order to give life, Hannah also travailed in order to produce life. In both of these incidences travailing meant pain, the anguish and struggle of a heart felt need for new life. Rachel travailed physically, emotionally, and spiritually to give birth to a son she wouldn't be able to hold, love, or keep. Hannah travailed physically, emotionally, and spiritually for a son to hold, love, and then give up.

Travailing is anguish; it is to feel the pain God feels over the lostness of men. It is to be burdened and broken over the sin in our lives that breaks God's heart. It is to weep over those who have rejected the claims of Christ on their lives and it is to hurt for those who are going through trials for Christ. Travailing is a joining of hearts with God, not that He must be conformed into our way of thinking, but that we would begin to know and yield to the will of God in ours.

> *We can no more have a revival without travailing then we can have salvation without the involvement of the Holy Spirit, it just cannot happen.*

Travailing in prayer for revival will mean tears; there cannot be any other way. Just as a woman in childbirth experiences the pain and tears of labor to bring forth life, we too, must experience the tears in order to produce new life. The tears are from a heart that God has broken and made sensitive to the moving of the Holy Spirit. They are also over the sin and rebellion that has been done and now seeks repentance. And the tears are a longing to experience the seasons of refreshing from the presence of the LORD again. We can no more have a revival without travailing then we can have salvation without the involvement of the Holy Spirit, it just cannot happen. David said, *"The sacrifices of God are a broken spirit; A broken and a contrite heart, O God, Thou wilt not despise"* (Psalm 51:17). I believe God is longing to send revival to His people, but it must begin individually, and it will involve travailing.

To be purposeful in our praying is a determination to see the Holy Spirit move in our hearts again, to revive us, and fill us with His love. It is a determination to travail in prayer until God sends a season of refreshing from the presence of the LORD. Persistent and purposeful prayer is the call to every believer who desires to see God move in and through their lives in order to bring revival, literally, another Pentecost.

Application:

Little did Jeremiah Lanphier realize when he began to organize a prayer meeting it would turn into a nationwide revival. He probably had no idea, as he prayed for revival, it would be like a match starting a forest fire. When he began to pray he probably had no concept God was about to use his prayer meeting to shake a nation for the cause of Christ. Jeremiah simply had a heart that cried for God. He wasn't the smartest, or the brightest, or the most successful in his field. He wasn't wealthy, or a man of power, or one of stature. Those who are of this persuasion are seldom used by God. No, Jeremiah was just an ordinary man God wanted to do some thing extraordinary with. We go back to James 5:16 and read, *"the effectual fervent prayer of a righteous man accomplishes much."* Jeremiah was made righteous by the blood of Christ and he lived a righteous life by the ministry of the Holy Spirit. When he travailed in prayer for a move of God within his North Dutch Reformed Church, God not only answered his petition but granted so much more.

When we pray, God wants to do far more in and through our lives than we can possibly imagine. We ask for small things because we view God as small. We pray occasionally and inconsistently and when there doesn't seem to be a response from God, we quit! Yet, do we really understand what it means to expect great things from God? We pray for daily bread when God wants to give us a warehouse. We ask for a soul to be saved when God wants to bring millions to His dear Son. We ask for a physical healing when God wants to pour out His Spirit in restoration, redemption, and healing. We pray for revival in our lives, God wants to set us on fire and revive a nation. In short, we ask our heavenly Father for pennies when He has billions to spare.

God wants to grant us seasons of refreshing from the presence of the LORD, if we will but meet the conditions. We talked about those conditions in chapter three with the repairing of the altar, the arranging of the wood, and the offering of the sacrifice. But there is one more requirement, and that is prayer. Elijah prayed and God sent the fire to consume the sacrifice. Elijah asked and expected great things from God, and God responded. Prayer is the one and only key that unlocks the power of God. Persistent, purposeful, fervent, travailing prayer of a righteous man can set the world on fire for the cause of Christ. It did in the past and it can again in the present. But will we have the faith to pursue prayer with all diligence? Are we willing to travail in prayer until we see God move in our hearts and then through us to the world? America's future and destiny may well depend on your prayers for revival.

In closing, Jesus, in Luke 18, taught His Disciples about being persistence in prayer and then left them with this challenge. *"Nevertheless when the Son of man cometh, shall he find faith on the earth,"* (Luke 18:8)? When Jesus comes will he find us with enough faith to be persistent, purposeful, fervent, and travailing in prayer? Think on these words to the great hymn, *"Teach Me to Pray,"* by Albert S Reitz and let this be our hearts cry.

Teach me to pray, LORD, teach me to pray;
This is my heart-cry, day unto day;
long to know Thy will and Thy way;
Teach me to pray, LORD, teach me to pray.

Living in Thee, LORD, and Thou in me;
Constant abiding, this is my plea;
Grant me Thy power, boundless and free:
Power with men and power with Thee.

Power in prayer, LORD, power in prayer;
Here mid earth's sin and sorrow and care;
Men lost and dying, souls in despair:
O give me power, power in prayer!

Living in Thee, LORD, and Thou in me;
Constant abiding, this is my plea;
Grant me Thy power, boundless and free:
Power with men and power with Thee.

My weakened will, LORD, Thou canst renew;
My sinful nature Thou canst subdue;
Fill me just now with power anew.
Power to pray and power to do!

Living in Thee, LORD, and Thou in me;
Constant abiding, this is my plea;
Grant me Thy power, boundless and free:
Power with men and power with Thee

Teach me to pray, LORD, teach me to pray;
Thou art my pattern, day unto day;
Thou art my Surety, now and for aye;
Teach me to pray, LORD, teach me to pray.

Living in Thee, LORD, and Thou in me;
Constant abiding, this is my plea;
Grant me Thy power, boundless and free:
Power with men and power with Thee (11)

Recall & Application

1.   To be persistent in prayer consisted of what three criteria?

_____

_____

2.   What two examples were used to explain travailing in prayer?

_____

_____

3.   What will "travailing in prayer" mean?

_____

_____

4.   What does it mean to you to travail in prayer?

_____

_____

5.   In what ways did the example of Jeremiah Lanphier speak to you?

_____

_____

6.   When God speaks, do I listen? God spoke to me in the following ways:

_____

_____

"Truly, truly, I say to you, unless a grain of wheat falls into the earth and dies, it remains by itself alone; but if it dies, it bears much fruit."

"He who loves his life loses it; and he who hates his life in this world shall keep it to life eternal." (John 12:24-25)

Chapter 10

The Call to Seasons of Refreshing
Death Produces Life.

Son, Come Back to Jesus:

There is a sign along Highway 19, going north out of
Nappanee, Indiana, which reads, *"Son, please come back to
Jesus."* It has been there for at least twenty years and no one
seems to know who put it there or to whom it was intended for.
It is a cry of a parent's heart longing for the return of their son
to an intimate relationship with the LORD Jesus Christ. It is the
burden of a mother who longs to see her son return to the faith
she patiently taught him. The prayers she labored for him when
he was sick and the Bible lessons she taught him at bedtime—
these are now distant memories, as the prodigal son goes off to
his own world. It is the heartache of a father longing to see his
son serve the living LORD and to live by the Biblical principles
he had taught and demonstrated to him. Now they both labor
intensely in prayer that God would move on the heart of their
prodigal child, desiring his return, first to the LORD and then
back to them. How many parents are pleading this same
phrase, *"Son/daughter, please come back to Jesus?"* The pain
a parent feels over the waywardness of their prodigal son or
daughter is devastating. Daily they ask what they could have

done differently to prevent this from happening. Yet, to each is given the freedom to choose their own lifestyle—servants of Christ or slaves to the devil and his world. As parents, we can plead with our children, we can show them, teach them, warn them, love them, and pray for them, but the decision for or against Christ is theirs alone. When they choose to walk away from the faith you so hoped they would follow, no amount of words can describe the hurt that is felt. *"Son, please come back to Jesus!"* It is a plea filled with tears from a broken heart, travailing in prayer, and yet—this is the most important thing that can be done. It is a dying to self in order to travail in prayer that life may be reborn.

The Prodigal's Father:

The story of the prodigal son (Luke 15:11-32) has a tremendous application for today. Previously, we discussed how the younger son came to his father and asked for his share of the inheritance. Once received, he packed his bags and journeyed to another country and spent everything he had on the sins of this world. During that time, scriptures were silent about the father of the erring boy. One can imagine the anguish he went through. The hurt and emptiness he must have felt, and the laboring in prayer he did on the boy's behalf. Everyday the father probably hoped this would be the day his son would return home. He longingly would look down the road, hoping to see a glimpse of his son and at the end of the day, when his son still had not returned, he would retire to bed with a heavy heart and a disappointed spirit.

The father was willing to do anything and pay any price in order to see his son return home. The father was willing to die to self in order to see life anew within his son. And so the father waited and longed for and prayed earnestly that his son would realize the love he had for him and return. Days turned into months, months turned into years, and the father continued to wait patiently. Each day the father would watch and pray, hoping and trusting the LORD to work in his son's heart, bringing him to repentance.

Many parents today are like the father of the prodigal son—waiting, hoping, and praying for the return of their son or daughter. They continually travail in prayer—dying to self in order that life may be born again within their erring child's heart. They know God has made every provision possible for their child to enjoy an eternity in the presence of the One who has loved and redeemed them. But they anguish continually and pray fervently, seeking God to bring brokenness to their child.

There is a happy ending to this story, as the prodigal son did recognize his need and returned home to his father and sought forgiveness. Scripture records while he was still a long way off, his father saw him and ran to embrace him. His son quickly said, *"I have sinned against heaven, and in thy sight, and am no more worthy to be called thy son."* (1) But the father would have none of that, for he embraced his son, kissed him, and loved him, for his son had returned home. The father's prayers had been answered!

Death had produced life. The father's travailing in prayer and waiting on God brought seasons of refreshing from the presence of the LORD, to his son and himself as well. *"Son, please come back to Jesus,"* now has become *"My son was dead and is now alive, was lost and has been found."* (2)

The Grain of Wheat:

"Truly, truly, I say to you, unless a grain of wheat falls into the earth and dies, it remains by itself alone; but if it dies, it bears much fruit." (John 12:24)

The grain of wheat is one of the smallest seeds in the agricultural community. It is hard to imagine from this one tiny seed a stalk of wheat can grow to produce massive amounts of grain. Each seed that falls to the earth and "dies" will produce a multitude of stalks, each producing an innumerous amount of seeds. If left to flourish without intervention, you would soon have a massive field full of precious wheat ready to yield an abundant harvest.

The Christian life is like a grain of wheat. If we are willing to die to self, God can produce within and through us life in

> *Dying to self is a disregard for personal rights in order that He may have the right to rule in our lives.*

abundance. Dying to self is not easy and it is not a once-and-for-all surrender at the altar. Dying to self is a moment-by-moment surrender to the will and call of God. It is an acknowledgement He is LORD of all we are or hope to be. Dying to self is a disregard for personal rights in order that He may have the right to rule in our lives. It is an abandonment of our comfortable, sinful lifestyle in order that He might make us uncomfortable about sin. It is a surrender of our leisure time so we may study more about Him in His Word. Dying to self is a giving up in order to gain.

To the unbelieving world, the idea of death producing life or dying to self is pure nonsense. But to the believer in Christ, it is a cry to be filled with the Holy Spirit, desiring more of Him and less of "me." John the Baptist, speaking of Jesus, told his followers, *"He must increase, but I must decrease."* (3) It is the Holy Spirit who calls us to surrender in order to conquer. He calls us to yield in order to become powerful and to be weak in order to become strong. These, which appear as a contradiction to the world, are truths to the believer because the Christian has the witness of scriptures and the teaching of the Holy Spirit.

The grain of wheat left alone will not produce fruit. It is only when it dies that fruit will be produced. It has to be broken and crushed in order to be turned into something of value and it has to be buried with heat applied in order to germinate, producing new life. Like the grain of wheat, the believer must be broken and crushed in order to be used and heat applied in order to grow. Wheat is life sustaining and valuable, a necessary part of our food chain that the world depends on. The believer, who is willing to die to self in order to produce life, is a necessary part of seeing revival come, and America's future depends on that.

Finding Life:

"He who loves his life loses it; and he who hates his life in this world shall keep it to life eternal." (John 12:25)

If we are to find life in its abundance, we must have hatred for the things that tear us away from our walk with the Savior. That which hinders our fellowship, the sin and desire to please self, must be put to death. Salvation is dying to the old self or lifestyle we once embraced and being created anew. Likewise, our daily walk with Christ is a continual dying to self and being filled anew.

> *To find life we must first be willing to loose it.*

To find life we must first be willing to lose it. It is more than putting to death the desires of the flesh constantly and continually. Rather, it is a dying to all of our ambitions, wants, and desires in order to obtain His. God's heart becomes our heart. His passion and burden for the lost and dying, becomes ours. And His love for others is our drive and determination. When we are willing to lose what the world calls *"life,"* then we will find true life in Him.

To lose one's life will mean striving in prayer over your prodigal child and it will mean praying in earnest for the lost and dying. This travailing or striving in prayer will be hard and painful, for someone you love dearly is on the road to sin and ruin. You will grieve over their condition and long for their return. Yet, you must remain steadfast in prayer, even though it may take years for them to come to the Savior. To lose one's life is to daily labor in prayer over the spiritual condition of the ones you love.

Losing one's life will also mean sacrifice—the willingness to pay any price in order to see lost people come to Jesus, to bear any burden in order to see revival come to your church, and the willingness to proclaim God's truth throughout the land. Sacrifice will involve giving, and not just money, but the most precious of all commodities, time. It takes time to labor in prayer, to minister, and to study in order to, *"show thyself approved unto God, a workman that needeth not to be ashamed, rightly dividing the word of truth."* (5) The ultimate sacrifice was demonstrated on the cross of Calvary where our Savior gave His life for all. Does He not ask the same from us? We think sacrificing is giving up an hour on Sunday to attend church, or to throw a few bucks into the collection plate as it passes by. We make comments about suffering for Jesus as we head for our next vacation paradise. The American Christian has no idea what sacrifice means! Christians throughout the Muslim parts of the world know the meaning of sacrifice for they do it daily. To proclaim Christ publicly in some countries is to have a death sentence placed on your head. Many have been beaten, tortured, and cast into prison for simply sharing the love of Christ. In Saudi Arabia, it is against the law to speak publicly of Jesus Christ, and yet many continue regardless of the consequences. In Vietnam, local pastors are often given the choice of renouncing Christ or face public beatings and imprisonment. In Sudan, attending a local church makes you a target for assassination. That's sacrifice! True life and abundant life, will come when we are willing *"to count all things but loss for the excellency of knowing Christ Jesus as LORD."* (6)

Losing one's life will mean surrendering, a letting go of all you hold dear. It may be letting go of your goals, dreams, finances, house, or your comfortable lifestyle in order for God to use you unhindered and yielding to His Lordship. Surrendering will also mean letting go of family members and allowing God to use them for His kingdom. Surrendering is difficult; letting go of our children is hard. But God plans for them are far greater than we can imagine and He desires to use them in ways we cannot understand. However, He desires a life surrendered, a willingness to say, *"Here's my heart, O take and seal it; Seal it for Thy courts above."* (4)

Losing one's life involves struggling in prayer, sacrificing, and surrendering. This doesn't sound very appealing does it? Yet, if we are to find true life in Christ, we must be willing to lose our own life for the cause of Christ. To the world, this too is a contradiction of terms, it just doesn't make sense! But to us who believe, it is the only way to experience true revival. It is similar to the grain of wheat that first must "die" in order to produce life.

Death produces life! Jesus was teaching His Disciples this concept by using the illustration of the grain of wheat. He would later use His own life as an example for all to understand the meaning of dying to self in order to produce life. He would challenge them and us with this statement, *"He that loves his life shall lose it."* Meaning, he who loves the things of this world far more than a relationship with Jesus Christ, will lose his life indeed. The prodigal son found this out after he wasted all of his inheritance on the sins of this world, only to end up feeding the hogs afterwards. His life, though pleasant for a season, was now miserable.

Hannah's example: (1 Samuel 1:1 -2:21)

To illustrate further how dying to self will produce life, there is a story in the Old Testament about a young wife named Hannah. She too, travailed in prayer and was willing to sacrifice everything in order to gain the desire of her heart. She knew also the meaning of surrender—to give up your most precious possession, in order to gain that, which cannot be lost.

I. Hannah's Barrenness:

We are told in 1 Samuel chapter one, that Hannah had no children and grieved continually as a result. Her name, Hannah, meant *grace* and she was barren of life—literally "grace unfulfilled." The desire of every Jewish woman was to give birth to a son, not only to help provide for the family when the parents grew older, but because their son could be the long awaited Messiah. Some looked at being barren with ridicule and disdain, as if it were a curse from God for a particular sin they might have done. Hannah faced this kind of contempt and it grieved her heart. She was barren of life and more than anything she wanted to bear a son, yet she was powerless to conceive.

The parents of a prodigal child often feel empty and barren of life because their child has wondered away from the faith. They too, often hear the ridicule and disdain from others over their child's waywardness. They feel powerless, unable to change the heart of their loved one. So they too, grieve.

II. Hannah's Brokenness: (1 Samuel 1:3-8)

Hannah wanted a son more than life itself, until finally it had produced within her a broken spirit. She wept continually and would not be consoled by her husband. We read her husband gave her a "double portion of blessing" he had received from his yearly sacrificial offering. What that consisted of we are not sure, but Hannah rejected it because her heart was broken over her barrenness. The desire of material blessings had no appeal. Even the desire for food was gone, as she wept and fasted. The love of her husband could not comfort her even though he tried, for her only desire was for a son. Hannah was dying in order to produce life. Her only desire, focus, and longing of her heart was for a son. Nothing, no comfort, no material blessing, no encouragement could change her heart. She would produce life or die!

If we are to see our prodigal children return to the LORD, we too must have the same broken spirit Hannah had. We must have a burning desire to see souls saved, the wondering prodigals returned, and our churches set on fire for Christ. Hannah wept and fasted, and would not be comforted until she received what she longed for. So also the church must weep and fast, refusing to be comforted until God moves in the hearts and lives of family members and friends that have ignored the claims of Christ.

III.   Hannah's Boldness: (1 Samuel 1:11-18)

Hannah, in order to gain a son, had to be first willing to give him up.

Scriptures record she went into the house of the LORD and cried out in bitterness of soul. *"And she made a vow and said, "O LORD of hosts, if Thou wilt indeed look on the affliction of Thy maidservant and remember me, and not forget Thy maidservant, but wilt give Thy maidservant a son, then I will give him to the LORD all the days of his life, and a razor shall never come on his head"* (1 Samuel 1:11). The vow she made was a Nazarite vow, stating the child would be raised as holy unto the LORD. Again, sometimes in order to gain life, we must first be willing to lose it. Hannah, in order to gain a son, had to be first willing to give him up. So she made a Nazarite vow, when her son would become old enough, he would be set apart for God's service for the rest of his life.

IV.   Hannah's Blessing: (1 Samuel 1:24-28)

Scripture records the LORD heard Hannah's prayer and granted her request. When the child became old enough, Hannah kept her word and presented him to Eli, the priest, in order to be trained and taught in the service of the LORD. Hannah died in order to produce life. She died to the things of this world in order to gain that which the world could not give, a son. When the child became old enough to do the LORD's work, she died again in surrendering him. But the LORD not only gave Hannah a son, He gave the nation of Israel one of the greatest prophets who ever lived. Her son, Samuel, faithfully served the LORD all of his life and was God's mouthpiece to a nation needing a righteous leader. Samuel would anoint two kings in his service. One king would become a failure in his actions and attitude. The other was King David who would unite a nation into a kingdom and be the lineage from which the Messiah would come. God blessed Hannah because she was willing to die in order to produce life. After she gave Samuel to the LORD's service, God blessed her with three more sons and two daughters.

God will bless those, like Hannah, who are willing to die to self in order to produce life and those who are willing to lose their life in order to find it.

Application:

The father of the prodigal son gave himself (died) in prayer so that his son would find life again. Hannah gave herself (died) in prayer to bear new life for God's service. Many Christian parents are giving themselves (dying) in travailing prayer for their erring children to find life anew in Christ. Believers in Christ must give themselves (to die) in earnest, heartfelt prayer, in order that our nation will return to Christ. It is the cry of our heavenly Father for America to repent and return in order for her sins to be forgiven and that times of refreshing would come from the presence of the LORD.

America may well be at a crossroad, and her destiny determined by the believers in Jesus Christ. On the one road is revival and restoration, a healing of the nation by the returning of the church of Jesus Christ to righteousness and holy living. On the other road is the pathway to total destruction, as God— in His righteousness—will judge this nation according to her sins. The church of Jesus Christ has been given a mandate, *"If my people, which are called by my name, shall humble themselves, and pray, and seek my face, and turn from their wicked ways; then will I hear from heaven, and will forgive their sin, and will heal their land"* (2 Chronicles 7:14). God will hear, forgive, and heal our land—it is death producing life! Are we willing to die to sin and self and earnestly seek Him?

The call to the church of Jesus Christ is like that sign along highway 19. *"Son, please come back to Jesus."* Only it is the cry of our heavenly Father saying, *"Church, please come back to Jesus,"* as He longs to pour out His Spirit afresh and anew on us. But, will we listen? Will we respond to the Holy Spirit's call to seasons of refreshing? How much further down the road to ruin will the church go before we, like the prodigal son, recognize our need and return to our Father in repentance? It is easy for the church to sit in judgment over the sins of an unbelieving world. But the unbelieving world acts sinful, because they are! They are simply responding to the sinful nature within them. The church of Jesus Christ is called to be the bearers of light and hope. We are to plead before God and with man that they might be saved. We too, should be responding to our new nature within us! However, if the church is sinful, who will do the pleading?

The call to seasons of refreshing is a call to die to self in order to produce life. Personal revival begins when we are willing to die to the world around us in order to experience new life in Him. Like the grain of wheat that first must die in order to produce life, so the Christian must die to self in order to bring forth life in others. This is seen in the example of the father to the prodigal son. How he must have labored in prayer, with weeping and fasting, over the lost condition of his child. God saw the brokenness of a father and pierced the heart of his prodigal son, bringing him home to be reconciled. If we are willing to die to self in order to pray in earnest, God will grant us new life. No one really knows how long the father prayed. But he was faithful, I believe, to seek daily the LORD, pleading for the life of his son, and God granted his request. We must remain faithful to the task of earnest prayer, of dying to self, and seeking God no matter how long it takes in order to see "prodigals" returned.

Hannah also died to self in order to bring forth life. She desired a son more than life itself and sought God with tears and fasting. God saw the travail of her soul and answered her prayer. God also sees the travail of our soul and will answer us as well. Hannah was broken and desperate for God to produce new life within her. We too, must be broken and desperate for God to produce new life through us.

The call to season of refreshing is a call to die to sin and live a holy and righteous life. God has told us in His word that the effectual fervent prayer of a righteous man will accomplish much (James 5:16). To see "much accomplished" in prayer is to die daily to sin and disobedience. When we die to self in order to give ourselves to prayer, God moves in and through us. Souls are saved, lives are transformed, and people are healed from sin and rebellion. If we long to see revival in our nation, we must first die to self. God sees the condition of our heart, whether we are proud and arrogant or broken and desperate. God responds to our prayers accordingly. If we are proud and arrogant, God will not hear and our prayers will go unanswered. What then will become of our nation, our communities, and our families? If we are humbled, broken, and desperate to see God move, He will grant us seasons of refreshing from the presence of the LORD. If we are to find life, we must first be willing to lose it!

As we close this chapter on the call to seasons of refreshing, consider the song written by Leila Morris, entitled *Nearer, Still Nearer*. It is an earnest prayer and longing of a heart to draw near to the Savior and find life in Him. Let this be your prayer as you contemplate on the words.

Nearer, still nearer, close to Thy heart,
Draw me, my Savior so precious Thou art;
Fold me, O fold me close to Thy breast,
Shelter me safe in that "Haven of Rest,"
Shelter me safe in that "Haven of Rest."

Nearer, still nearer, nothing I bring,
Naught as an off'ring to Jesus my King;
Only my sinful now contrite heart,
Grant me the cleansing Thy blood doth impart,
Grant me the cleansing Thy blood doth impart.

Nearer, still nearer, LORD, to be Thine,
Sin, with its follies, I gladly resign;
All of its pleasures, pomp and its pride,
Give me but Jesus, my LORD crucified,
Give me but Jesus, my LORD crucified.

Nearer, still nearer, while life shall last,
Till safe in glory my anchor is cast;
Thro' endless ages, ever to be,
Nearer, my Savior, still nearer to Thee,
Nearer, My Savior, still nearer to Thee. (5)

Recall & Application

1.   In what ways is the Christian life like the grain of wheat?

_____

_____

2.   If we are to find true life in Christ, we must first be willing to do what?

_____

_____

3.   Losing one's life will involve three things; what are they?

_____

_____

4.   Hannah's example consisted of four things, describe them?

_____

_____

5.   What does it mean to die to self?

_____

_____

6.   When God speaks, do I listen? God spoke to me in the following ways:

_____

_____

And the word of the LORD came to me saying, "Son of man, behold, I am about to take from you the desire of your eyes with a blow; but you shall not mourn, and you shall not weep, and your tears shall not come. Groan silently; make no mourning for the dead. Bind on your turban, and put your shoes on your feet, and do not cover your mustache, and do not eat the bread of men."

So I spoke to the people in the morning, and in the evening my wife died. And in the morning I did as I was commanded. And the people said to me, "Will you not tell us what these things that you are doing mean for us?"

Then I said to them, "The word of the LORD came to me saying, 'Speak to the house of Israel, "Thus says the LORD GOD, 'Behold, I am about to profane My sanctuary, the pride of your power, the desire of your eyes, and the delight of your soul; and your sons and your daughters whom you have left behind will fall by the sword. 'And you will do as I have done; you will not cover your mustache, and you will not eat the bread of men. 'And your turbans will be on your heads and your shoes on your feet. You will not mourn, and you will not weep; but you will rot away in your iniquities, and you will groan to one another.
'Thus Ezekiel will be a sign to you; (Ezekiel 24:15-24)

Chapter 11

The Final Plea for Seasons of Refreshing
I'll take away the Desire of Your Eyes

When my children disobeyed I usually corrected them with a word of warning; when they continued to disobey certain punishment resulted. We've all done this, but what do you do when your child is an adult and living in disobedience? As a parent, you hurt for them and grieve over their rebellious nature. You wonder what it is going to take to awaken them out of their sinful lifestyle and return to the LORD. Many parents pray that God will bring something into their child's life to shock them back into reality. They are desperate to see their child return to a walk of obedience to the LORD. And sometimes desperate people do desperate acts in order to achieve their desires.

God was about to do a desperate act in order to awaken His erring people. Ezekiel was a prophet sent by God, to the people of Jerusalem, to warn them of certain judgment if they didn't repent and return to the LORD their God. God had used Ezekiel to give various signs, illustrations, and warnings to the people—but still no repentance. Finally, in an act of desperation, as a final plea, God gave Ezekiel one last sign to the people. This sign was the hardest of all messages Ezekiel had to convey. It was a final plea for revival and this message the church of Jesus Christ must heed as well.

Ezekiel's Sign:

This final message to the people of Jerusalem and Judah is found in Ezekiel chapter 24, and it took place prior to the final siege by Nebuchadnezzar, King of Babylon, in July of 586 B.C. It was a last ditch plea from a loving heavenly Father to His wayward people to repent and return in order that their sins would be forgiven and that times of refreshing would come from the presence of the LORD. (Acts 3:19) Impending doom awaited if they did not heed the message and understand the sign given to them by Ezekiel. Nebuchadnezzar was an exceptionally cruel king and he would not spare the people in Jerusalem, and most assuredly, would loot and destroy the temple of all her treasuries. It was the Father's last plea from a broken heart as if to say, *"Son, please come back to Jesus."*

I. I'll Take Away the Desire of Your Eyes:

"And the word of the LORD came to me saying, "Son of man, behold, I am about to take from you the desire of your eyes with a blow; but you shall not mourn, and you shall not weep, and your tears shall not come. "Groan silently; make no mourning for the dead. Bind on your turban, and put your shoes on your feet, and do not cover your mustache, and do not eat the bread of men." So I spoke to the people in the morning, and in the evening my wife died. And in the morning I did as I was commanded." (Ezekiel 24:15-18)

This is a sobering story to contemplate, as it deals with the death of Ezekiel's wife. He was commanded not to weep publicly, nor shed a tear in front of the people. He wasn't allowed to put on the mourner's clothes or eat the food friends brought to comfort Ezekiel in his time of loss. He was to die to self in the midst of his personal grief in order to convey a desperate plea for life. He was commanded to put on his turban and shoes as if it were a normal day. And so Ezekiel went out to speak to the people in the morning as usual and in the evening his wife died. The next morning, he did just as he was commanded. Why would God use the death of Ezekiel's wife as a sign of impending judgment? Why would God use such drastic actions? Can you imagine how Ezekiel's heart must have been broken over the death of his dear wife? He had loved and depended on her for comfort and encouragement, now she was gone.

> *He literally was to die to self, in the midst of his personal grief, in order to convey a desperate plea for life.*

In understanding this sign, we must first know the heart of God. He is a loving heavenly Father who aches over the sin and rebellion of His people. Sometimes desperate situations call for desperate measures and the final call to the people of Jerusalem had to be dramatic in order to get their attention. How it must have broken God's heart to do this to His faithful servant. But it often takes a tragedy to awaken people to their own personal accountability. The shock value of the death of someone usually provokes responses from some; when Ezekiel went about business as usual—this had to bring a lot of questions.

Ezekiel, as a prophet, is first married to God and He becomes the center of his life, the desire of his eyes, and the longing of his soul. A prophet must first be willing to be broken and poured out before God in order to be used by God to witness before men. He must be willing *"to count all things but loss for the excellency of knowing Christ Jesus as LORD."* (1) And he must be willing to die daily in order that Christ may live in and through him. Ezekiel must grieve privately, but to the people he must show forth the message God has given him. The message, in the illustration of the death of his wife, was a picture of what was going too happened to them.

II. You will do as I have done:

"And the people said to me, "Will you not tell us what these things that you are doing mean for us?" Then I said to them, "The word of the LORD came to me saying, 'Speak to the house of Israel, "Thus says the LORD GOD, 'Behold, I am about to profane My sanctuary, the pride of your power, the desire of your eyes, and the delight of your soul; and your sons and your daughters whom you have left behind will fall by the sword."

'And you will do as I have done; you will not cover your mustache, and you will not eat the bread of men. 'And your turbans will be on your heads and your shoes on your feet. You will not mourn, and you will not weep; but you will rot away in your iniquities, and you will groan to one another."

"Thus Ezekiel will be a sign to you; according to all that he has done you will do; when it comes, then you will know that I am the LORD GOD."' (Ezekiel 24:19-24)

The people were at a loss to understand the behavior of Ezekiel, who wouldn't be? He had lost his wife—the desire of his eyes—and there wasn't any outward display of mourning. There wasn't the usual loud wailing or lamentations done, customary for the day, nor the large gathering of family and friends coming to pay their respects. Out of desperation they cried out,

> *But righteousness will be vindicated either through repentance or judgment and this was their final warning!*

"*tell us the meaning of all this?*" But did they really want to know the answer? Do we?

The message was devastating! God was about to remove the desire of their eyes. First, God would desecrate His temple, which was the pride of their power. The Temple was the holiest place on planet earth, for there God dwelt and met with His people. They must have thought, surely God would not do this to His temple. But righteousness will be vindicated either through repentance or judgment and this was their final warning! This message alone should have been enough to bring revival in the land as their confidence was in the presence of God in His temple. To profane the temple would mean God would abandon His presence with them, thereby allowing

Gentiles to overrun the Holy Place. It was a warning that God was withdrawing His hand of protection and giving them over to the King of Babylon. Their power and strength would be gone, they would be defenseless as the LORD of Hosts would no longer defend them. The pride of their power became a building and not a holy life before God. They trusted in what the temple stood for rather than following the holy commands of God. God had promised He would bless them if they obeyed and curse them, if they did not. Now the pride of their power, the temple, was going to be profaned by a Gentile king who was vicious and cruel and had no thought or care about burning it and leaving it in ruins.

Secondly, the desire of their eyes was their sons and their daughters. Many would be killed and those left would be carried off to Babylon as slaves. Nebuchadnezzar showed no pity regardless of age or sex of the individual. He had no need for the very young or the old as he either left them to the elements or ran them through with a sword. The desire of their eyes and the delight of their soul, their children, would be taken away with a blow, killed before their very eyes! What a tragic warning with devastating consequences! Can you see why God used such drastic measures to warn His people?

God, in His love, was using the death of Ezekiel's wife to warn the people of Jerusalem to repent and return before it would become too late. This final message to His people was from a broken heart of a loving LORD who longed to send revival instead of ruin, life instead of death, hope instead of despair, and seasons of refreshing instead times of destruction. But did they listen? The sad answer is, as history bears out, they did not and Nebuchadnezzar did as he pleased with the temple and the people. The devastation lasted for seventy years! Jerusalem was reduced to ruble and the temple was ransacked and burned, thousands of people died and the rest were carried off to captivity to be slaves to the nobles of Babylon.

Application:

There is an axiom, which says, *"Those who will not learn from history are doomed to repeat it."* I think of the destruction of Jerusalem and the years spent in captivity in Babylon, and wonder how far off America is from facing her Babylon. I wonder what drastic measures God will use in order to call His church back to seasons of refreshing? When I read of devastating earthquakes, hurricanes, tornadoes, or floods that have hit various communities, I wonder is God using these calamities to wake up His church? Could these events be a final plea from God for revival?

> *Yet, during this holocaust of the unborn, the church has remained silent and Christians continue to vote for political candidates who support the slaughter of the innocent.*

The church of Jesus Christ must acknowledge and repent of all sin while there is still time. There cannot be a hiding of "secret sins" and we can no longer try to rationalize or justify our wretched behavior before a Holy God. Instead we must fall at His feet for mercy. God is willing and wanting to forgive and restore. However, if we refuse what drastic measures will He apply?

Is the message of Ezekiel applicable for today? Consider the following fact that over 1.6 million babies are aborted in America every year. Since Roe vs Wade in 1973, over 40 million unborn children have been killed in the womb. (2) Add to that the tragedy of partial birth abortion, where a child is killed as it is being born, and you have a Holy God crying out, *"the voice of thy children's blood crieth unto Me from the ground."* (3) Can a Righteous God not hear the cries of the innocent without bringing retribution? Yet, during this holocaust of the unborn, the church has remained silent and Christians continue to vote for political candidates who support the slaughter of the innocent.

But there is more to consider. The breakup of the American family continues unabated. In 1994 there were 1,191,000 divorces granted leaving 18,590,000 children in a single parent home. (4) Recently a judge lamented about the divorce cases he had witnessed. He stated when he entered into the Judiciary, almost all custody arrangements went to the mother of the children. In the 1980's, the father starting getting custody of the children, as the mother didn't want the responsibility. Now, neither of the parents want the responsibility of raising their children, leaving the courts with the unenviable tasks of finding suitable homes for them. He went on to lament that the most dangerous place for a child to be today is in its own home! Is it any wonder we are raising a generation that does not have a soul—literally, not knowing or caring about right from wrong? Divorce in the church has reached an all time high, equaling that of the secular world. The church again, has remained silent on speaking out against the growing trend of divorce among its members; choosing to look the other way and often remarrying couples who have had multiple divorces. Daily we hear of pastors or leaders in the church having adulterous affairs with no remorse shown. Listen very closely to the Word of God through Malachi the prophet, *"For I hate divorce," says the* LORD, *the God of Israel.* (5) Yet, in our churches today, little is spoken in regards to God's hatred of divorce because it isn't politically correct and it's considered divisive.

There are even more issues to consider. Pornography has become a multi-billion dollar industry and now can be accessed into your living room via computer. The Internet today contains some of the most shocking and graphic depictions of pornography one can imagine. When concerns are raised about who is watching this and what are the effects on them, we are reminded by the ACLU of the first amendment right of freedom of speech. Many Christians are enticed into and addicted to pornography and it will take the power of God to set them free. But, they must recognize their need and want to repent and return in order for deliverance to come. The sad truth is many believers are happy and content with their sin, and that becomes scary indeed.

In 1992 there were 1,932,274 violent crimes committed and these were the ones actually reported. (6) The Psalmist said, *"The wicked shall be turned into hell, and all the nations that forget God."* (7) That, is just what many of our inner cities have turned into, a living hell. They are filled with crime and rampant drug abuse leaving many with the feelings of hopelessness, trapped in their environment and unable to get out. The only hope for our inner cities is revival in the church, moving believers out of their comfortable pews and into the mission field of the hopelessly lost with the good news of Christ. It will take a mighty move of the Holy Spirit, setting on fire the churches in order for them to become lighthouses amidst the darkness. It will take the power of the Holy Spirit to push back the forces of hell in order to see the violent come to Christ for salvation. But it can be done and God wants to do it, will we seek Him for it?

Many churches have pushed to normalize homosexuality by marrying gay couples and ordaining homosexual priests and ministers. Choosing to ignore God's strict warning against such practices, many have openly condoned, accepted, and now endorsed such behavior. God still calls it a perversion and an abomination. We seem to forget that the Biblical cities of Sodom and Gomorrah were destroyed for such practices. There is also the continual scandal in politics, as the church again chooses to ignore sin in high places. When the former President of the United States was exposed for his perversions and numerous affairs, few of our church leaders cried out for his resignation. Many simply agreed with the liberal philosophy that character doesn't matter as long as the President governs by the will of the people. Ezekiel's message is a warning to the church today and it may be the final plea for seasons of refreshing.

Ezekiel's message was one of dire consequences revolving around three distinct judgments. First, God would remove their spiritual pride, the temple would be looted, burned, and left in ruins; gone would be the worship through the sacrificial offerings. Secondly, God would remove their national pride. Their King and the freedoms they possessed would be taken away and they would become strangers and aliens in a foreign land. And third, God would take away their family pride. Their sons and daughters would fall by the sword or be taken into captivity. Before all this would happen, God gave them one more warning in the sudden death of Ezekiel's wife. That which had happened to her would surely happen to them if they did not repent and return to God.

Could it be that God's warning to America is the same, beginning with God removing our spiritual pride, the freedom to worship, pray, and study God's Word openly? Already in many parts of our country it is illegal to gather for home Bible study based on vague zoning laws. Many are threatened with

> *Never before in the history of the United States has there been the capability of a few to bring down so many with one act of terrorism.*

lawsuits if they pray before organized sports outings, commencements, or with a student in need. Bibles are forbidden to be carried to school or the work place and Christians are mocked on television shows, movies, and on the radio. We have gone from being called a Christian nation to a secular nation in just a few decades. Is God removing our spiritual pride as a way of humbling us to return to Him?

Secondly, God is removing our national pride, the ability to defend ourselves against foreign and domestic enemies. Many feel America faces imminent danger within her own borders, as terrorism has become an actuality and not just a possibility. Today there is the threat of chemical and biological agents being released unto the unsuspecting public as an act of terrorism. Never before in the history of the United States has there been the capability of a few to bring down so many with one act of terrorism. The carnage from the destruction of the twin towers in New York City, on September 11, 2001, could be just the beginning of what is about to happen. The next time, literally, cities could vanish under the holocaust of a nuclear explosion. Could it be God is removing our national pride as being a military leader in order for us to call out to Him for His protection and strength?

Thirdly, God is removing our national pride as the economic

> *We are losing our sons and daughters to alcohol and drug addiction. We are losing our sons and daughters to materialism, sexual promiscuity, and secularism. And we are losing our sons and daughters in all forms of decency because that is what we have taught them.*

leader in the free world. This past year, the stock market has and continues to be volatile, short rallies are followed by lengthy downturns. Many have lost thousands of dollars in the roller coaster ride of the stock market. Major company stocks have plummeted and earnings have declined throughout most of the fiscal year. Daily the newspapers are full of stories of massive layoffs and companies downsizing. They say a recession is when your neighbor loses his job, a depression is when you lose yours. Add to this that the average American is loaded with personal debt and you have the makings of a catastrophe on hand. Conservative estimates state that the average person has over $8,000 in credit card expenditures. If the economic bubble bursts, how will the average American pay their bills with that much debt? Could it be that God is removing our national pride as an economic leader in order for us to again trust in Him for His blessings and provisions?

Lastly, God is removing our family pride with the loss of our sons and daughters. If America is involved in another regional conflict, particular the Middle East, it will be our sons and daughters that will be in harms way and this time the casualties could be enormous. But there are other ways to lose our sons and daughters than in a war. Our children see our inconsistencies in matters of faith, church attendance, scripture reading, and in a holy walk with God. They see our inappropriate lifestyle, hear our perverse speech, and witness our dishonest gain. They think to themselves, if it isn't real with mom and dad why do I need it? Add to that the continual assault by secular institutions that God is no longer a viable option and it is no wonder that we are one generation away from extinction as a people of faith. We are losing our sons and daughters to alcohol and drug addiction. We are losing our sons and daughters to materialism, sexual promiscuity, and secularism. And we are losing our sons and daughters in all forms of decency because that is what we have taught them.

The three forms of judgment God had warned the people of Jerusalem through Ezekiel, the prophet, are happening within America today. How far will it go? How severe will the chastening become? What will be the results? These are all questions that can be answered by the believer. At what point in time will he or she repent and return to the LORD, their God?

This is a call from God to every believer to experience seasons of refreshing from the presence of the LORD. This call continues to go forth just as the father pleaded with his prodigal son to, "please come back to Jesus." God in His love and mercy is pleading with every believer in America today to turn from sin and experience His fullness, as they have never experienced it before. The Apostle Paul in the book of Romans gives us this challenge, *"And that, knowing the time, that now it is high time to awake out of sleep: for now is our salvation nearer than when we believed. The night is far spent, the day is at hand: let us therefore cast off the works of darkness, and let us put on the armour of light. Let us walk honestly, as in the day; not in rioting and drunkenness, not in chambering and wantonness, not in strife and envying. But put ye on the LORD Jesus Christ, and make not provision for the flesh, to fulfill the lusts thereof."* (Romans 13:11-14 KJV) Knowing the time, we have the witness of history—we can see current events and understand that time is running short. We truly need to cast off the deeds of darkness and put on the armor of light.

This plea to seasons of refreshing could very well be our last call. Like the warning from Ezekiel with the tragic death of his wife the shock value eventually wears off and we return to our old ways. However, there is another alternative. If we will heed the call to seasons of refreshing, if we will return to a personal revival with the LORD our God, He will pour out His Spirit afresh and anew upon us. We can experience His love and forgiveness in ways we've never known before and we can draw close in an intimate relationship with the LORD Jesus Christ. The choice is ours! The choice is yours! God is pleading with you now, *"Son, please come back to Jesus."* Will you come?

To those who continue to have a close personal walk with the LORD Jesus Christ—the call to seasons of refreshing is a call to labor in prayer. As Ezekiel pleaded with his people to repent, we must pray for our people, our churches, our communities, and our nation to humbly seek the LORD God for mercy and forgiveness. Like the father of the prodigal son who longed for the return of his son, we must long for and earnestly pray that our Heavenly Father will once again send a revival to sweep through our churches.

The call to seasons of refreshing begins with surrendering, a yielding of one's life to the Lordship of Jesus Christ. In the quietness of your heart maybe you would like to repeat this prayer.

"Oh gracious Father, I have sinned. I have called that which is evil in Your sight as good. And I have called that which is good, as evil. Forgive me and cleanse me of all my iniquities and create in me a clean heart. Holy Father, I would ask that you break my heart for the things that break yours. That I would see the lostness of men as you see them, and I would love them as You loved them and gave Yourself for them. Father, use me, break me, fill me with Thy precious Holy Spirit and cause me to be yielded to Your leading. Precious

Father, send us seasons of refreshing from the presence of the LORD and begin that work within me. I surrender all to you, dearest Jesus. Take my life and use it for Thy glory. There is no price I will not pay, or sacrifice I will not make in order to see You glorified within my life, my family, my community, and literally my nation again. Thank you precious Father. In Jesus precious name, Amen!"

Recall & Application

1.   What did God tell Ezekiel that He would take away with a single blow?

_____

_____

2.   Why, do you think God had to use such drastic measures?

_____

_____

3.   What was the message that God was conveying through the example of Ezekiel's wife?

_____

_____

4.   In what ways to you see Ezekiel's message as one for today?

_____

_____

5. In what ways is God speaking to America?

_____

_____

6.   When God speaks, do I listen? God spoke to me in the following ways:

_____

_____

Therefore, just as the Holy Spirit says, "TODAY IF YOU HEAR HIS VOICE, DO NOT HARDEN YOUR HEARTS AS WHEN THEY PROVOKED ME, AS IN THE DAY OF TRIAL IN THE WILDERNESS," (Hebrews 3:7-8)

"For we have become partakers of Christ, if we hold fast the beginning of our assurance firm until the end; while it is said, "TODAY IF YOU HEAR HIS VOICE, DO NOT HARDEN YOUR HEARTS, AS WHEN THEY PROVOKED ME." (Hebrews 3:14-15)

Epilogue:

Seasons of Refreshing
How Then Should We Live?

How Then Should We Live?

The Chinese have a proverb, which states that, *"The journey of a thousand miles begins with the first step."* Throughout this book, we have talked about seasons of refreshing, a returning to a personal revival with God. The challenge is up to you to take the first step into seasons of refreshing. The first step is found in Acts 3:19, *"Repent therefore and return, that your sins may be wiped away, in order that times of refreshing may come from the presence of the LORD."* We have talked about repentance throughout the chapters, but let's examine this verse more closely and understand what it means for us today.

I. Repentance:

Repentance means to turn, to change direction, and to think differently. Turning involves a change in lifestyle, as old habits must be broken and new ones made. Sins can no longer be excused, blamed on someone, or justified based on extenuating circumstances. They must be confessed and forsaken. To change direction will mean a new course or a new walk on a different pathway. The old paths will no longer be traveled on for those are the roads that led to sin and rebellion. This new course will lead to life and peace. To think differently will mean to focus on the Lordship of Jesus Christ, and to let His word fill our thoughts and control our actions.

Repentance is necessary for salvation because it is an acknowledgement that the pathway or the course of life we were on was wrong. Repentance is necessary to personal revival because it acknowledges we have strayed off the right pathway and onto one, which leads to sin and ruin. Repentance is admitting before God that our actions, attitude, and lifestyle are nothing more than sin and rebellion before Him. Remember 1 John 1:9 states, *"If we confess our sins, He is faithful and righteous to forgive us our sins and to cleanse us from all unrighteousness."* This is the promise we have in Christ, for He is quick to forgive and cleanse us from all our transgressions.

II. Godly Sorrow:

Repentance involves Godly sorrow for the sins that have distanced us from fellowship with a Holy God. David said, *"The sacrifices of God are a broken spirit; A broken and a contrite heart, O God, Thou wilt not despise"* (Psalm 51:17). David was broken over the sin in his life that grieved God and he expressed a deep sorrow for it. David clearly acknowledges he was wrong and didn't try to excuse it away, *"Wash me thoroughly from my iniquity, And cleanse me from my sin. For I know my transgressions, And my sin is ever before me.*

Against Thee, Thee only, I have sinned, And done what is evil in Thy sight" (Psalm 51:2-4). Godly sorrow is a sincere heart crying out to God for mercy and grace in times of need. David was pleading with God to be washed and made clean again. He didn't try to justify his behavior or cover up his sin. He acknowledged the fact that his sin was before God, for nothing can be hidden from Him. Therefore, God was justified in His accusations and blameless in His reproach.

David was called a "man after God's own heart." Have you ever wondered why? It was David adulterous affair with Bathsheba that led to the murder of her husband, Uriah, and brought disgrace upon the name of God throughout the land. David's life was full of mistakes, blunders, and bad decisions. Yet God honored David with this title. Why? The answer is found in the brokenness of David, as seen in Psalm 51. Let's look at a few examples.

"Purify me with hyssop, and I shall be clean." (v.7a)

The Hyssop plant was used by the priest to sprinkle blood around the altar, as a ceremonial act of cleansing and purifying. What David was pleading for was to be cleansed by the blood of the lamb. You and I have the blood of the Lamb of God where we can go to for forgiveness and restoration.

"Wash me, and I shall be whiter than snow." (v. 7b)

David asked God to wash him of his sins and iniquities in order to be clean again. His desire was to be made white as snow, literally, brilliantly white as a snow filled day. When we repent of sin and seek forgiveness there is no greater feeling than being cleansed. The weight of guilt and conviction is lifted, fellowship is restored, and once again intimacy with God is available to us. We are made clean and pure in God's eyes again.

"Create in me a clean heart, O God, And renew a steadfast spirit within me." (v. 10)

David was not asking for repair of his old heart, nor was he asking for a band-aid to cover the wounds. He was requesting God to create in him a clean heart, for a new heart will not go back to the sin that brought this reproach in the first place. Peter likens it to a dog returning to his vomit, (1) which is totally disgusting to see. The visual will help illustrate how God feels about us returning to the same sin we have just repented of. A renewed spirit will cause us to focus on making sure we do not return.

"Do not cast me away from Thy presence," (v. 11a)

Many of the Psalms reflected the joy David found within the presence of God. Yet, David knew that sin separates fellowship with a Holy God and in order for fellowship to be restored—sin must be repented of and forsaken. Our desire is to be in constant fellowship with our LORD Jesus, to be filled with and used by the Holy Spirit. But in order to have or maintain that fellowship, we must have a sensitive heart toward sin and the things that grieve God's heart.

"And do not take Thy Holy Spirit from me." (v. 11b)

This was a petition, that as believers in Christ, we will never have to pray, because God has given the Holy Spirit to abide in us forever. (2) We can grieve the Holy Spirit with our sin, as Paul tells us in Ephesians 4:30, and we can quench the Holy Spirit from using us, as Paul again state in 1 Thessalonians 5:19. But God will not take away that which He has promised would be the seal of our future redemption. In the Old Testament times, the Holy Spirit came upon believers at random for special anointing. David, realizing this, didn't want to lose the Holy Spirit's leading and filling because of his sin.

These are just a few examples found in Psalm 51 typifying David's heart of repentance. This is the reason why God called him a man after His own heart. David had a sensitive heart toward sin and he sought forgiveness and restoration when he went astray. It is important to note throughout Psalm 51, David does not seek justification for his actions. He doesn't shift his sin onto someone else, nor does he conceal the matter once God has brought him under conviction. He was open and honest before God admitting, *"I have sinned and done this evil before a Holy God."* If we are to have a repentant heart, we must be open and honest before God as well. Take note of Psalm 51—this is a picture of a heart broken over sin. If we are to have a personal revival, to experience seasons of refreshing from the presence of the LORD, we must view sin as David did—with brokenness and contrition.

III.   Returning:

Repentance is a change in the course we are taking. Returning means to come back to where we once were. There is an indication here of having left someone or something, and we have. We've left our fellowship, our intimacy, and our walk with our loving heavenly Father. When we repent, we acknowledge our sin and turn from it. When we return we come back into fellowship and enjoy intimacy with God. Once again, we desire His Word in our lives and we focus on times of prayer and fellowship with Him. We long to be used by Him, to encourage others, to reach the lost; once again, we want to unite with God's heart that His will be accomplished in and through us.

Returning is a renewing of our commitment to Jesus Christ. It is similar to a couple on their anniversary—renewing their wedding vows—as they promise to continue their love and devotion for one another. It is a commitment made out of love with a sincere heart and a single purpose, which is faithfulness. Renewing our commitment to the LORD Jesus Christ is a rededication of our love and devotion to Him. It is to again faithfully follow and serve Him with a sincere heart and single purpose that He might be glorified in all we do.

Returning is an acknowledgment of His Lordship; that He is LORD indeed of all I am or hope to be. It is understanding and acknowledging that a part from Him I can do nothing. Jesus said in the Gospel of John, *"I am the vine, you are the branches; he who abides in Me, and I in him, he bears much fruit; for apart from Me you can do nothing."* (3) If I am to bear fruit in the ministry God has called me to, and if I am to live a life pleasing to Jesus, I must yield to His Lordship. It has been said Christ is either LORD of all or He is not LORD at all. Therefore, when we yield to His Lordship, we begin to understand that when in submission and subjection—we can find strength.

Returning is an act of humiliation, as it involves surrendering of pride. Whether one comes to an altar at a church or alone on his face before God, it is a time of sweet surrender. It doesn't matter what others may think or say as long as God hears and restores. When we humble our self in His presence, there must be a willingness to make right the wrongs we have committed. This will involve seeking forgiveness and making restitution where needed. Even though the price may be high, the blessings will be worth it. God uses the humble spirit of an individual—after making restitution—to be His witness of salvation. I have seen marriages restored and family relationships healed because a father was willing to humble himself before God and seek restoration. Revival has broken out in churches because individual members have sought forgiveness from those they have wronged. I have seen individuals freed from guilt and bondage they carried because they humbled themselves and sought forgiveness from those they have wronged over the years.

God is calling out to His church to come back, to return before it is too late. Many believers have lost their first love for Jesus. They may be active in their local church, faithfully serving and ministering in various capacities—but they are just going through the motions. The love for this world has replaced the love they once had for the risen LORD. Some have said that they want to experience all the world has to offer before returning to Jesus Christ. But no one is guaranteed of tomorrow and for some...they have run out of tomorrows. Now is the time to repent and return to the LORD our God. The writer to the book of Hebrew's said, *"Therefore, just as the Holy Spirit says, Today if you hear His voice, do not harden your hearts."* (4) When God moves on the heart of an individual—calling them to repent and return—the plea is don't harden your heart! Don't become obstinate and rebellious! Scripture states, *"Take care, brethren, lest there should be in any one of you an evil, unbelieving heart, in falling away from the living God."* (5) The hardening of the heart will lead one to fall away from the living God, so guard your heart!

IV.   That your sins may be wiped away:

"Repent therefore and return, that your sins may be wiped away."

God desires to forgive sin and to cleanse from all unrighteousness. He wants to remove the guilt and frustration sin causes and to bring deliverance from the habitual practice and bondage to sin. David said, *"How blessed is he whose transgression is forgiven, Whose sin is covered! How blessed is the man to whom the LORD does not impute iniquity, And in whose spirit there is no deceit!"* (Psalm 32:1-2) David knew the joy of being forgiven and cleansed because he repented and returned to the LORD God. No matter how grave the sin may be or how long you have harbored it, God is willing and wanting to forgive and cleanse you, but the decision is yours. You can continue to harbor sin and not know the joy and peace of forgiveness or you can repent and return in order that your sin may be wiped away. David said, *"When I kept silent about my sin, my body wasted away through my groaning all day long."* (6) David felt the physical consequences of sin and was greatly troubled until he acknowledged his transgressions. Then he experienced the peace of God that filled him with songs of praise.

V. Times of refreshing from the presence of the LORD:

"In order that times of refreshing may come from the presence of the LORD."

Times or seasons of refreshing from the presence of the LORD has been the focus throughout this book. We have talked about the desperation for seasons of refreshing, the direction to seasons of refreshing and the determination of seasons of refreshing. Each topic leads us to repentance and to return so that God would forgive our sins and grant us seasons of refreshing from His presence.

Seasons of refreshing is God filling His people with a renewed source of power. It is the Holy Spirit again giving us boldness in our proclamation of the good news of Jesus Christ. We, then, can face uncertainty with calmness and faith because of that power in us.

The Holy Spirit's power will also revive our prayer lives, as we come before the throne of grace with a sense of urgency and expectation to see God move in the hearts of people. He will teach us to pray, and pray through us when we struggle and are not sure how or for what to pray. He will also empower us to push back the forces of darkness, as we pray in order that souls may be captured for Christ and lives changed forever.

Seasons of refreshing is God filling His people with a new sense of His presence. It is the Comforter within, giving us guidance, wisdom, and strength for each day. His presence

> *It is His presence that brings comfort during difficult times, hope during times of despair, and praise in times of victory.*

gives us a new heart for worship and adoration for who He is and what He has done in and through us. There is a new desire to draw close to Him through His Word as we devote ourselves to study and meditation. His presence creates a sensitive heart enabling us to listen to the still small voice of God. It is His presence that brings comfort during difficult times, hope during times of despair, and praise in times of victory.

Seasons of refreshing is God filling His people with a new strength of purpose as we become determined to be used by Him for His honor and glory. We will seek greater challenges, broader horizons, and more difficult tasks because He will deepen our faith and we will grow. We can no longer be satisfied with the mundane Christian life, as we desire to attempt great things for God and to be used greatly by God. Our single focus is Jesus Christ, for He is the longing of our soul and serving Him is the desire of our heart. The Psalmist said, *"Delight thyself also in the* LORD; *and he shall give thee the desires of thine heart."* (7) Our delight and longing will be to go where He leads and accomplish what He asks us to do. For some, it will be a mission field, for others it will be into full time Christian ministry. Some will serve the LORD along with their vocation, while others will serve by giving and supporting those who go. Some will see a great harvest of souls and some will pay the ultimate price for their labor. But for all, the desire of their heart will be to hear the Master say, *"Well done, Thou good and faithful servant: thou hast been faithful over a few things, I will make thee ruler over many things: enter thou into the joy of thy LORD."* (8)

When God Moves: The Church's Wake up Call to Seasons of Refreshing.

It was a quite, peaceful morning on September 11, 2001. I was on my way to Medina, Ohio, traveling on the 80/90 turnpike. There was a cool breeze from the north, as the season began to change from the warmth of the summertime to the delightful colors of autumn leaves. But on this day, life in America would never be the same. Like the sudden attack on Pearl Harbor on December 7, 1941, the United States was suddenly changed forever with a new Pearl Harbor on September 11, 2001. The death toll will probably never be fully known, as thousands lay buried underneath tons of concrete and steel from the once tall and magnificent structures that stood. Among the masses of dead were the passengers and crew of the four planes that were hijacked and used as cruise missiles slamming into the twin towers, the Pentagon, and the grassy field in Pennsylvania. It is America's wake up call to terrorism; it is the churches wake up call to prayer and revival.

The daily papers screamed with the headlines, *"Are We Ready For War?"* The answer is quiet assuredly, NO! We are not prepared to see the suffering and casualties of war. We are not prepared for the hardships produced by war and we are not prepared to make personal sacrifices for the cause of war. We as

Americans have had it too good for too long. Our riches and our high standard of living have become our curse when God meant it for a blessing. Our peace and security have made us greedy and lazy when God wanted us to reach the ends of the world with the Good News. And our freedom and liberty have become license for perversion and immorality when God meant it for spiritual growth and evangelism. Now we may be facing the prospects of a long war against terrorism. What we have feared most may become a reality—more attacks and carnage in the streets of our nation.

This war will be different than any in America's past, for this involves enemies we cannot readily identify. They are secretive and move in and out among friends who give comfort and aid and then deny any knowledge of their whereabouts. It may also involve an enemy we've depended on to keep our economy going with precious oil, and it may be one we have armed and trained in the past.

This war will involve our sons, and now—our daughters, as America has sought to become "more diverse" regardless of the consequences. My friend told me he was troubled at the thought of his daughters being called off to war, and the prospects of them becoming causalities. I know what he is thinking, for I am a father of three very precious daughters myself and it is troubling indeed to contemplate their future.

This war will be costly, not only in terms of dollars spent, but in lost freedoms, as politicians—seeking homeland security and more votes—shred the constitution. Security will be tightened, people will be watched, phones will be tapped, e-mails will be read, and "religious people" will be considered fanatics. The church of Jesus Christ may well face the watchful eye of the ever encroaching government, as they seek to curtail large gatherings and shun the prospects of evangelism. Laws will be passed—marking those who disagree with the government as suspected terrorists.

This war will be devastating in terms of lost lives and carnage done. Retaliation and counter retaliation could lead to more acts of terrorism drawing the whole world into a global conflict. The threat of weapons of mass destruction being used either by terrorist or us is very real indeed. Are we ready for such devastation? No. Who could be?

Our Hidden Enemy.

To the believers in Christ, we also fight a similar enemy. One who attacks suddenly and with stealth. An enemy who has no thought for those he has injured or destroyed, and no pity on the carnage he has caused, or the souls he has taken. He has no compassion for the wounded and broken hearted, and no sense of remorse for the evil and harm he has done. He has wealth untold, power beyond human understanding, and resources unimagined. He seeks to be honored and worshipped as the prince of this world, the ruling force behind kingdoms and authorities. He speaks and commands, and his army instantly obeys, without question or consideration for the acts done. He is moving the world ever closer to Armageddon with fanaticism, lies, and deceit he spreads unhindered. His greatest weapon is deception. If he can prevent people from finding the truth and applying it to their lives, then they will walk in darkness and he will control them forever. He has deceived kings, presidents, rulers, priests, prophets, and ordinary people into believing he doesn't exist. He has infiltrated churches and caused splits and divisions. He has watered down the Gospel, making it weak and ineffective. He has created discord among the faithful and saturated the clergy with perversion and lust. He has removed Bibles from countries, tribes, communities, schools, businesses, and even churches. He has perverted the translations by removing paragraphs, sections, and verses in the name of making it more readable for modern man. In the name of diversity, he has encouraged perversion, liberalism, and feminism with the purpose of destroying the family unit. Knowing that in doing so he will ultimately weaken the nation and destroy it from within. He has changed laws and customs from that which was considered wrong and sociably unacceptable, to now being accepted, endorsed, and promoted. He specializes in temptations bringing all kinds of addictions to the easily persuaded and the weak, thereby, binding their souls in a living hell making it impossible to escape from. He is the master of all evil, wicked, and abdominal. The enemy has a name, he is Satan and his purpose is to keep believers from repentance and seeking God in prayer for times of refreshing. The last thing Satan wants, and to which he will fight against with every ounce of his being, is to have believers earnestly and fervently seek the living LORD for revival. This war has been waged everyday since the Garden of Eden, and it will end victoriously with the coming of the King of kings and LORD of lords, Jesus Christ.

Believers must realize Satan is alive and well on planet earth and cannot be brought to justice. Rather, he must be defeated. His defeat will only happen when believers earnestly and fervently seek the LORD Jesus Christ in prayer and repentance. The time for revival is now! The wake up call has been sounded! The survival of our nation is at stake and it rests upon us, the believing remnant.

In times of despair and disaster, many will turn to the church of Jesus Christ looking for answers and seeking hope. The church must be prepared for the onslaught and be ready *"to make a defense to everyone who asks you to give an account for the hope that is in you."* (9) The church must become the beacon of light in the coming times of darkness that is about to sweep our nation. Like lighthouses from another era, piercing the darkness with their ray of light and bringing guidance and hope to many weary sailors, so must the believing church of Jesus Christ provide the light of God's Word.

This is a wake up call to the believing church to prepare for a different war. One that will be fought on the battlefields of prayer, with the weapons of a broken and contrite heart, calling out to our LORD Jesus Christ to forgive our sin and heal our

> *This is a wake up call to the believing church to prepare for a different war. One that will be fought on the battlefields of prayer, with the weapons of a broken and contrite heart, calling out to our LORD Jesus Christ to forgive our sin and heal our land.*

land. It is a battle that every believer must participate in, there can be no exceptions. The enemy is strong and determined but, *"You are from God, little children, and have overcome them; because greater is He who is in you than he who is in the world."* (10) We have the forces of heaven at our disposal, the Word of God at our command, and the power of the Holy Spirit within. We can, indeed, overcome the enemy. The battlefield of prayer will be hard fought as the enemy has long been entrenched and it will take persistent, earnest, and fervent prayer to dislodge him.

God, at times, allows tragedies to take place in order to waken His children. He has done this in the past with the nation of Israel. Many times they wandered away from God in sin and idol worship. God would then punish His people by allowing a foreign army to invade. Israel would repent and seek God for deliverance and He would provide the victory. He often used ordinary people to accomplish this, men like Joshua, Barak, and Gideon, along with David, who had his mighty men of valor. These were just ordinary people who sought God during times of national trials and God used them to bring deliverance and restore hope to the people. This tragedy can be turned into triumph if we, like Israel did in the past, call out to God for His mercy and deliverance. What Satan has meant for evil and destruction, in order to bring about his purpose and plan, God can take and turn for the good. In the past, He has taken tragedy and turned into triumph, He has taken ashes and turned into riches, and He has taken death and created life. Joseph said to his brothers' years after they had sold him into slavery and left him for dead, *"As for you, you meant evil against me, but God meant it for good in order to bring about this present result, to preserve many people alive."* (11) What others have done at the beckoning call of Satan to do evil, God can turn it into a nation-wide revival.

God can take the tragedy that has happened to this nation and turn it into a mighty move of drawing many to the LORD Jesus Christ for salvation. Already He has planted the seeds. Others will come and water, and soon there will be a harvest, a harvest of souls for the Kingdom of Heaven. The believing church must not shrink back from the call to be witnesses for our LORD, as now more than ever before hearts are open and prepared for the Gospel. When God moves on the hearts of the lost they will seek other believers for answers and we must be ready to share the truth of God's Word. They will seek out growing churches filled with the Holy Spirit, as they desire to know more about Jesus and to learn from His Word. Many have earnestly prayed for years to see a mighty move of God on the lost, to see one more great harvest of souls before the Rapture, and God may be preparing hearts for just that.

God can take this tragedy and turn it into a mighty move of God within His Church. Many have also prayed for revival, a turning back to personal faith and obedience in the LORD Jesus Christ. God is using these events to call His church back to Him, back to prayer and repentance, back to preaching and studying God's Word, and back to holy living and heart for worship. Already many churches have started or renewed their mid week prayer service with large crowds participating. When God moves on the hearts of His children, they will pray in earnest.

When God moves on the hearts of people—souls will be saved, lives will be changed, believers will repent and return and the faithful will pray. This tragedy may turn into the greatest spiritual triumph in the last one hundred years. America has not experienced a nation-wide revival since the Great Awakening of 1858-1859. This may be just the beginning of times of refreshing from the presence of the LORD. Let's pray that it is and that it will continue.

Summary and Application:

Seasons of refreshing are lessons on personal revival. It is a call for believers to repent and return to God so we may experience times of refreshing from His presence. It is a call to the lost, who may be reading this book, to repent and turn to Jesus Christ. It is a call to come, *taste and see that the LORD is good:"* (12) To taste, means to experience all the magnificence of His goodness and mercy; to chew or meditate on the richness of His promises; and to digest all the wonderful nutrients of His Word.

God is waiting and longing for you to come unto Him. He wants to cleanse and purify, He desires to forgive and renew, and He longs to heal and restore. He is not willing that any should perish but that all would come unto repentance. (16) He desires to fill you with His Holy Spirit and empower you to live a victorious Christian life. He wants to consume you with His love and presence so that you may know Him in all of His fullness.

God, similar to the father of the prodigal son, is waiting patiently for your return. He has pleaded with you through His

> *The desperate long for a moving of God in their lives, because they are hungry and thirsty for righteousness. Personal revival is what they seek and plead for from God.*

Word, He has pricked your heart with His Spirit, and He has pierced your soul with His unfathomable love. The still small voice of the Holy Spirit is crying out to you, *"Son/daughter, please come back to Jesus."* His grace is sufficient to cover your deepest sin and His mercy knows no limits in forgiveness. He is our loving Heavenly Father who is filled with compassion for the destitute, comfort for the abused, hope for the downtrodden, strength for the weak, and mercy to the needy. Will you call out to Him today? Will you seek Him for forgiveness and restoration? Will you call out to Him for mercy and salvation?

God is looking for those individuals who are desperate for Him in order that He may consume them with the fire of His love. The desperate long for a moving of God in their lives, because they hunger and thirst for righteousness. Personal revival is what they seek and plead for from God and they desire His cleansing from all sin. They earnestly seek the filling of the Holy Spirit, and to be used in ways they have not known before. They desire seasons of refreshing from the presence of the LORD, because apart from him, they are empty and barren of life. The desperate cannot be turned away, discouraged, or detoured. They have set their heart on seeking the risen Christ and nothing can persuade them to change their minds. The desperate look with anticipation for the coming of their King of kings and LORD of lords and they live each day in the light of His return. These are the characteristics of the desperate, as they long for the presence of God to fill their lives again. Are you one of the desperate? Do you long for the presence of God in your life again? If so, then call out to Jesus and earnestly seek Him in prayer and in His Word. Remember we have the promise of His Word, *"And ye shall seek me, and find me, when ye shall search for me with all your heart. And I will be found of you, saith the LORD:"*(12)

God is looking for those individuals who are not only desperate for Him, but are determined by Him to see revival begin in their churches, communities, and ultimately their nation. They are determined to be persistent and purposeful in prayer until God moves. They are determined to pray, because they understand the seriousness of the situation the church is in. They desire to pray, because God has placed the burden of revival on their hearts and they are directed to pray by the leading and filling of the Holy Spirit. They are determined to see God move on the hearts and lives of individuals, leading them to repentance and restoration in order that times of refreshing may come from the presence of the LORD. Are you one of the determined? Will you begin to earnestly and fervently seek the LORD until He sends and spiritual renewal throughout the land? We also have this promise to claim, *"If my people, which are called by my name, shall humble themselves, and pray, and seek my face, and turn from their wicked ways; then will I hear from heaven, and will forgive their sin, and will heal their land."* (18) Will you claim this verse in prayer until God brings healing to our land?

Finally, God is looking for those individuals who are not only desperate and determined, but also disciplined. The disciplined will not quit or grow faint during the times of trial, because they have prepared themselves for hard times. The disciplined will not be led astray or entangle themselves with the cares of this world. They are like soldiers in battle, trained and obedient, following every command of their LORD. The disciplined are prepared to give their lives for Christ, for they know death produces life. Finally, the disciplined will not grow weary in praying for seasons of refreshing, because they have a promise to claim as well, *"And let us not be weary in well doing: for in due season we shall reap, if we faint not."* (19) Are you one of the disciplined? Will you daily seek the LORD in prayer for revival?

The desperate long for God, the determined seek after God, and the disciplined are prepared to sacrifice everything for God. How then shall we live? We live with a sense of desperation for seasons of refreshing in our lives. We are determined to see God bring seasons of refreshing to our lives. And we are disciplined to the pay the price for seasons of refreshing through our lives. May God grant us times of refreshing from His presence again.

"Father, I long to see a mighty move of God in and through my life. LORD Jesus, I am desperate for You because I realize apart from You I can do nothing and I am nothing. I'm desperate for Your cleansing of sin in my life; for Your filling of the precious Holy Spirit; and for Your power to be used through me to touch others. Oh God, here is my life, sinful as it is, but wanting to be cleansed, restored, and used by You and for Your glory. Father, here I am, and I long to do Your will.

Here I am, I'll obey Your every command. Here I am determined to seek You until You bring times of refreshing from Your presence. Here I am, LORD, Here I am. In Jesus name, Amen."

Recall & Application

1.   **What does repentance mean to you personally?**

_____

_____

2.   **What areas has God spoken to your heart that you need to repent of?**

_____

_____

3.   **What does it mean to you to be desperate for God?**

_____

_____

4.   **What areas in your life are in drastic need of spiritual discipline?**

_____

_____

5.   **How are you going to apply 2 Chronicles 7:14 to your life?**

_____

_____

6.   **When God speaks, do I listen? God spoke to me in the following ways:**

_____

_____

Bibliography:

Chapter One:

1. Psalm 139:23-24
2. Matthew 6:21
3. Mark 8:36-37
4. Matthew 6:21
5. Matthew 16:26
6. *Shadow Of The Almighty,* The Life and Testament of Jim Elliot. By Elisabeth Elliot. Zondervan Publishing House, © 1958.
7. Chapter 10, Stress and Health from the book *Exploring Psychology,* by David G. Myers. Worth Publishers, 1999. Article, *The Stress Response System,* page 369.
8. Ibid. page 371
9. Ibid. page 375
10. Matthew 6:21
11. Romans 8:32
12. 1 Timothy 1:7
13. Hebrews 4:16
14. *Have Thine Own Way, Lord!* By Adelaide Pollard. Favorite Hymns of Praise, Tabernacle Publishing Co. copyright © 1978.

Chapter Two:

1. Compton's 99 Encyclopedia Deluxe, Program Discs. Copyright 1998, The Learning Company, Inc.
2. John 4:14
3. *Matthew Henry's Commentary On The Old Testament.* Electronic Editing STEP Flies. Copyright © 2000, Parson's Technology, Inc. Cedar Rapids, Iowa. All rights reserved.
4. Jeremiah 15:16
5. Psalm 29:2
6. Jeremiah 29:13-14
7. Mark 4:39
8. Psalm 30:5

Chapter Three:

1. Compton's 99 Encyclopedia Deluxe, Program Discs. Copyright 1998, The Learning Company, Inc.
2. Ibid.
3. 1 Kings 17:30
4. Ephesians 5:3
5. Ephesians 5:5
6. Exodus 20:3
7. Revelation 2:4-5
8. Hebrews 4:12
9. Joshua 7:1-26
10. *Are You Washed In The Blood,* by Elisha A. Hoffman. Favorite Hymns of Praise, Tabernacle Publishing Co. copyright 1978.
11. I Kings 17:2-16
13. John 11:1-44
14. II Chronicles 16:9 KJV
15. *Revive Us Again*, by William P. Mackay. Favorite Hymns of Praise,
Tabernacle Publishing Co. copyright 1978.

Chapter Four:

1. Compton's 99 Encyclopedia Deluxe, Program Discs. Copyright 1998, The Learning Company, Inc.
2. *A Shepherd Looks at Psalm 23,* by Phillip Keller. Ppg 115. Zondervan Publishing House copyright © 1970.
3. John 10:14
4. Psalm 121:4 = *The Holy Bible, King James Version.* Electronic Edition STEP files Copy right © 1998 Parson's Technology, Inc. Cedar Rapids, Iowa. All rights reserved.
5. 1 Peter 5:8 = *The Holy Bible, King James Version.* Electronic Edition STEP files Copyright © 1998 Parson's Technology, Inc. Cedar Rapids, Iowa. All rights reserved.
6. John 10:10

7. James 4:7 = *The Holy Bible, King James Version.* Electronic Edition STEP files Copyright © 1998 Parson's Technology, Inc. Cedar Rapids, Iowa. All rights reserved.
8. 1 Peter 5:7
9. Matthew 18:12-13
10. 2 Corinthians 1:3-4
11. Philippians 4:19
12. Psalm 103:5
13. Philippians 4:11
14. Luke 15:11-32
15. 1 John 1:9
16. James 1:5
17. Psalm 145:18
18. II Timothy 1:7
19. 1 Corinthians 15:54-55
20. Hebrews 4:12
21. Matthew 24:35
22. II Peter 1:3
23. Isaiah 26:3-4
24. Ephesians 5:18
25. *Savior, Like a Shepherd Lead Us*, by William B. Bradbury. Favorite Hymns of Praise, Tabernacle Publishing Co. copyright © 1978.

Chapter Five;

1. John 1:12
2. Matthew 11:23-24
3. 1 Kings 19:10
4. 1 Kings 18:39
5. 1 Kings 17:17-24
6. 1 Kings 19:3
7. 1 Kings 19:8
8. 1 Kings 19:9
9. 1 Kings 19:10
10. 1 Kings 19:18

11. Colossians 2:9-10; Scripture taken from the *New King James Version.* Copyright © 1979, 1980, 1982 by Thomas Nelson, Inc. Used by permission. All rights reserved.
12. Psalm 46:10; Scripture taken from the *New King James Version.* Copyright © 1979, 1980, 1982 by Thomas Nelson, Inc. Used by permission. All rights reserved.
13. Philippians 4:5-6
14. Philippians 1:6
15. James 1:22
16. 2 Timothy 2:15; *The Holy Bible, King James Version.* Electronic Edition STEP files Copyright © 1998 Parson's Technology, Inc. Cedar Rapids, Iowa. All rights reserved.
17. Joshua 1:8
18. Isaiah 32:17
19. Adam Clark's Commentary On The New Testament, by Adam Clark. LL.D., F.S.A., ETC. PARSONS TECHNOLOGY, INC. CEDAR RAPIDS, IOWA.
20. *Jesus Is Calling,* by Fanny Crosby. Favorite Hymns of Praise, Tabernacle Publishing Co. copyright © 1978.

Chapter Six:

1. *The Works of Josephus,* by Flavius Josephus. Electronic Edition STEP Files Copyright © 1998 Parsons Technology, Hiawatha, Iowa. All rights reserved.
2. 2 Chronicles 26:1-23
3. Psalm 135:18
4. Ezekiel 1:26
5. John 12:41
6. 1 Kings 8:27
7. Ezekiel 1:13
8. Isaiah 64:6
9. Revelation 3:17
10. *America Is Too Young To Die, A Call to Revival* by Leonard Ravenhill. Copyright © 1979 Leonard Ravenhill. All rights reserved. Published by Bethany Fellowship, Inc. Minneapolis, Minnesota
11. 1 Peter 4:17

12. The Holy One of Israel is used 29 times throughout Isaiah
13. *Sodom Had No Bible,* by Leonard Ravenhill. Copyright © 1971 Leonard Ravenhill. All rights reserved. Published by Bethany Fellowship, Inc. Minneapolis, Minnesota
14. John 14:16-17
15. 1 Corinthians 6:19
16. Jeremiah 29:13-14
17. *Majestic Sweetness Sits Enthroned,* by Samuel Stennett. Favorite Hymns of Praise, Tabernacle Publishing Co. copyright © 1978.

Chapter Seven:

1. Luke 24:49
2. John 14:12
3. Acts 2:3
4. Exodus 19
5. Midrash is a traditional Jewish interpretation of Scripture.
6. Weissman, Moshe, The Midrash Says: Shemot, Broolyn: Bnay Yakov Publications, 1995
7. *Sodom Had No Bible*, Leonard Ravenhill, Copyright © 1971 Leonard Ravenhill. All rights reserved. Published by Bethany Fellowship, Inc. Minneapolis, Minnesota.
8. *Sodom Had No Bible*, Leonard Ravenhill, ppg 153. Copyright © 1971 Leonard Ravenhill. All rights reserved. Published by Bethany Fellowship, Inc. Minneapolis, Minnesota
9. Acts 4:13
10. Romans 1:16
11. Acts 4:31
12. Acts 3:10-11
13. Acts 5:16
14. Acts 2:47
15. Acts 5:28
16. John 4:23-24
17. Matthew 5:13
18. *Fill Me now*, by Elwood H. Stokes. Favorite Hymns of Praise, Tabernacle Publishing Co. copyright © 1978.

Chapter Eight:

1. Genesis Chapter 3
2. Proverbs 6:16-17
3. Galatians 5:16
4. Matthew Chapter 4
5. Galatians 5:22-23
6. 2 Samuel chapter 11
7. Matthew 14:23-31
8. John 14:15
9. Romans 8:16-17
10. 1 Peter 1:3-4
11. Ephesians 6:10-15
12. 2 Timothy 2:15
13. Psalm 69:18
14. Psalm 69:19
15. Daniel 6:15
16. Genesis 39:9
17. *More Holiness Give Me,* by Philip P. Bliss. Favorite Hymns of Praise, Tabernacle Publishing Co. copyright © 1978.

Chapter Nine:

1. *The Fervent Prayer: The Worldwide Impact of the Great Awakening of 1858.* By J. Edwin Orr. Moody Press, 1974.
2. Ibid. Page 6.
3. Ibid. Page 10
4. Ibid. Page 10
5. Ibid. Page 11
6. Ibid. Page 12
7. Ibid. Page 14
8. Ibid. Pages 21-22
9. John 14:16
10. *Teach Me To Pray*, by Albert S. Reitz. Favorite Hymns of Praise, © 1978 Tabernacle Publishing Company.

Chapter Ten:

1. Luke 15:18-19
2. Luke 15:32
3. John 3:30
4. Favorite Hymns of Praise, © 1978 Tabernacle Publishing Company. *Come Thou Fount, Robert Robinson.*
5. Favorite Hymns of Praise, © 1978 Tabernacle Publishing Company. *Nearer, Still Nearer, Leila N. Morris.*

Chapter Eleven:

1. Philipians 3:8
2. *Storm Warning, the Coming Persecution of Christians and Traditionalists in America,* by Don McAlvany. Hearthstone Publishing, Oklahoma City, Oklahoma. © 1999 page 30.
3. Genesis 4:10
4. *The Choice America at the Crossroads of Ruin and Revival,* Sammy Tippit. Moody Press, © 1998.
5. Malachi 2:16
6. Sammy Tippit, Ibid.
7. Psalm 9:17 (KJV)

Epilogue:

1. 2 Peter 2:22
2. John 14:16
3. John 15:5
4. Hebrews 3:7-8a
5. Hebrews 3:12
6. Psalm 32:3
7. Psalm 37:4
8. Matthew 25:21
9. 1 Peter 3:15
10. 1 John 4:4
11. Genesis 50:20
12. Jeremiah 29:13

To Order Extra Copies of:

Seasons Of Refreshing:

The Hunger For Spiritual Renewal

Contact Jerry Hunt at the following:

E-Mail

jlhunt52@hotmail.com

or visit our Web Site at
www.seasonsofrefreshing.com

Special discount applies for quantities over 10.

About the Author:

Jerry has been a Bible teacher for over twenty-five years. He has successfully organized and developed various ministries ranging from college and career age to adult Sunday school classes. He has preached from various pulpits and served in numerous capacities at the local church level. Currently, Jerry teaches a Sunday school class at Nappanee Missionary Church, Nappanee, Indiana. As a business consultant, he held numerous seminars on a variety of topics including financial independence, time management, and consultative selling. He has written and produced training manuals for various companies. Jerry is a graduate from Indiana University with a BA in Sociology. Jerry and his wife Pat have four children, and live in Bremen, Indiana.

Printed in the United States
1203300002B/49-510

9 781410 755452